THE EMPIRE AND THE FIVE KINGS

THE EMPIRE AND THE FIVE KINGS

America's Abdication and
the Fate of the World

Bernard-Henri Lévy

Translated by Steven B. Kennedy

A Holt Paperback
Henry Holt and Company   New York

Holt Paperbacks
Henry Holt and Company
Publishers since 1866
120 Broadway
New York, New York 10271
www.henryholt.com

A Holt Paperback® and ® are registered trademarks of
Macmillan Publishing Group, LLC.

Originally published in France in 2018 by Éditions Grasset

Library of Congress Control Number: 2019286159

ISBN 978-125-02-3130-7 (trade paperback)

Our books may be purchased in bulk for promotional, educational, or business
use. Please contact your local bookseller or the Macmillan Corporate and
Premium Sales Department at (800) 221-7945, extension 5442, or by e-mail at
MacmillanSpecialMarkets@macmillan.com.

Originally published in hardcover in 2019 by Henry Holt and Company

First Holt Paperbacks Edition 2020

Designed by Kelly S. Too

CONTENTS

THE EMPIRE AND THE FIVE KINGS

On Dove's Feet, the Kurds

WHEN I REVIEW THE REASONS WHY, AT THIS STAGE OF MY LIFE, I poured so much energy into the cause of the Kurds and Kurdistan, this is what comes to mind.

The justice of the fight, of course.

The greatness of this people, whose claims to self-government are so much more solid than those of so many others in the region.

I am not a fanatical believer in nation-states. But the least one can ask of the world is that it be consistent in its principles. There exists in the Middle East a state, Syria, that emerged from the decisions of a Franco-British diplomatic duo whose job was to divide the spoils of the Ottoman Empire. The same dignity has been conferred on another lethal fiction with no true identity, Iraq—and this exemplifies the logic of cold-blooded monsters. But in the Kurds we have a people possessing solid and long-standing grounds for asserting their rights. A great people who have paid for their determination to endure with a mountain of suffering rare in human history. Should they be told that they are not a people, are superfluous, and lack standing to demand the independence that, for more than a century, has been the dream and the glory of their fathers? *This*, to me, violates the notion of the most basic fairness.

Next, there is the debt they are owed. The indelible debt that the world owes to the only armed force that, when ISIS appeared and the region was frozen stiff with terror, dared fight it face-to-face. It was because I was aware of this debt that I, with a small band of friends, came to the region between July and December 2015 to shoot a documentary film, *Peshmerga*, along the six-hundred-mile front that the Kurds were holding, alone, against the fanatics of the Islamic State. It was because I was aware that these men and women—the Peshmerga includes battalions of women—were the first line of defense not only of Kurdistan but of the world, that I left Europe again in November 2016, on the first day of the fight for Mosul, to make a second documentary, *The Battle of Mosul*, about the liberation of the most important city of the Caliphate. And it was for the same reasons that I personally promoted these films wherever anyone was willing to show them, that I brought the first of them to the very symbolic great hall of the United Nations building in New York and to the hallowed dome of Congress in Washington, and that I lived those two years in step with the Peshmerga and their aspirations. These fighters were sentinels against barbarism, the world's outposts and shields. The film crew and I deemed it essential to be the witnesses of that.

Another of the reasons for my commitment is the fight for an enlightened Islam, which, as I grow older, I realize has been one of the major concerns of my life. At age twenty, it led me into the rice paddies of Bangladesh; then, forty years later, into the Libyan desert. It took me into Commander Ahmad Shah Massoud's Afghanistan in defense of the Dari people, the heirs of Rumi, Hafez, and *The Roses of Ispahan.* Into the Pakistan of the torturers of Daniel Pearl and of those who, from Lahore to Karachi, mourned him as a brother. It had previously plunged me into Sarajevo and held me there for the nearly four years of the Serbian war, where the Islam of tolerance and peace was inspiring the Bosnian resistance fighters and their leader, Alija Izetbegović. It brought me back to Algeria, the land of my birth, at a time when illiterate emirs were sowing terror and the men and women who were resisting the deadly poison of Islamism (sometimes from outside the faith but more often from within it) needed ideological ammunition and encouragement. It was only logical that the same battle, the same desire to make a difference in the war of civilizations that pits the Islam of the learned against the Islam of the assassins should guide me one day into the mountains where the Kurds put their faith in democracy and law, in equality of women and men even on the field of battle, in secularity, in the diversity of faith, and in the sacred obligation to protect Christians, Yazidis, Shiite Muslims, and Jews.

Abiding with me during those seasons spent with the Kurds was a preference for the tangible, which, since my university days, I have always viewed as the most reliable guardrail against systemic thinking, the fatal temptation of those enamored of thought. The phenomenology of Edmund Husserl; Jean-Paul Sartre's affection for the substance of things; and Polybius, the historian on horseback, present at the siege of Carthage, who thought, like Heraclitus, that the "eye" is greater than the "ear," that an "autopsy" is always more valuable than a "testimonial," and that, to write history, it is best to have lived at least a little of it. Polybius, who, as we were taught in the elite French preparatory classes of the last century, had but one adversary to whom he devoted an entire volume of his *Histories*: the illustrious Timaeus, whose work has been lost but whom Polybius viewed as the prototype of the recumbent historian, the bookworm, the library rat, who never faced danger or fatigue while compiling the stories of others. I was on Polybius's side at the time. And when I decided early on to witness the living theater of man's cruelty with my own eyes whenever possible, I was thinking of Polybius as much as I was of Ernest Hemingway, of the

Russian novelist and war correspondent Vasily Grossman, or of the photographer Lee Miller. Nearly a half century later, I have not changed my mind.

And finally there is the taste for distant adventures that, like my preference for the tangible, grew with me into adulthood and accounts for the fact that I have never been able to rank a thinker, however fertile his mind, above the type of writer that a great French resistance fighter, Roger Stéphane, called "the adventurer" in a short work, *Portrait de l'aventurier* (with a preface by Jean-Paul Sartre), that was one of the breviaries of my generation. For me, those adventurers include, once again, strategists such as Polybius, who was said to be an expert in encrypting signals and could calculate the exact height of the ladders needed to scale a fortress from the shadows its walls cast on the ground; men of action like T. E. Lawrence, who brought his mad conquest to a culmination in the monument of sand and dreams that was *The Seven Pillars of Wisdom*; the Hemingway of *By-Line*; writer-combatants like George Orwell in Catalonia or André Malraux in his Latécoère airplane in Spain or Romain Gary in his Boston bomber of the Lorraine squadron; writer-mercenaries like Xenophon, who put his art of war to work for Cyrus the Great and who, from the protracted retreat of the Ten Thousand, drew the material for that bible of lost causes that is *Anabasis*; the ascetic Byron of Missolonghi; and the splendid Maurice de Saxe, who was regaled with a great play drawn from the repertory and mounted in his campaign theater on the eve of his victories at Prague and Fontenoy, and who gave the very Rousseau-like title of *Reveries* to his treatise on the art of war.

Time passes. The models persist. They abided in me as I argued to the Kurdish president, Massoud Barzani, that entering Mosul and planting his flag would be as decisive for his people as was the taking of Aqaba for Faisal's tribes in World War I. And they were still on my mind as I followed the long, dusty Kurdish columns into the Sinjar Mountains and as I bivouacked in the Zartik Mountains with Maghdid Harki, the young, white-haired Peshmerga brigadier general, brave but so vulnerable, whom I vainly tried to convince to reinforce the roof of his bunker. At least I was able, in my film, to chronicle his final moments.

I HAVE WRITTEN ELSEWHERE ABOUT SOME OF THESE REASONS. One day I may return to them at greater length.

But there was one last reason, perhaps the most important, and it accounts for this book.

At the end of these two years of adventure I witnessed the unfolding of an event that, upon reflection, is quite extraordinary.

President Barzani, the head of the Peshmerga, had come to believe that the time for unrequited sacrifice was over and that the moment had arrived to remind the international community of the promise made to the Kurdish people a century ago, in the letter and spirit of the treaties of Sèvres and Trianon that brought World War I to a close in the Middle East.

Therefore, in September 2017 he took the initiative of organizing a referendum that, as he emphasized over and over again, from Sulaymaniyah to Erbil, would *not* be followed by a unilateral declaration of independence.

He insisted that its true purpose was to begin a dialogue with the federal state of Iraq, in Baghdad, which had long since ceased to observe all but a fraction of its constitutional and budgetary obligations with respect to the Kurds.

How did the federal power in question respond to this offer of dialogue?

With a series of punitive measures, followed by a total blockade of Kurdistan, followed in turn by a full-fledged invasion in early October of the Kirkuk region, the oil capital of the country.

And in response to that invasion, in response to the surprise offensive planned in secrecy in Tehran and Baghdad, in response to an attack of ten against one (and, as if that were not enough, of tanks against men), what was the position of Kurdistan's historic allies, its sister democracies, which, only days before, could not heap enough praise on the Peshmerga?

They could find nothing to say.

They uttered not a word as Kurdish houses in Kirkuk were gassed and ransacked, women raped, people tortured.

Not a word as our comrade and cameraman Arkan Sharif was left to bleed to death, a kitchen knife stuck in his throat.

And, after Kirkuk was taken, as the tanks advanced on Erbil, the international community, the United States foremost, lifted not a finger to forestall or foreshorten this outrage; only by throwing all of their forces into the battle, and with their backs to the wall, did the Peshmerga succeed in protecting Erbil.

This is certainly not the first time that such a betrayal has occurred.

And through family lore, recent memory, and, in this latest episode, direct experience, I know that there is a suicidal weakness in the relationship between the democracies and war; that our first reflex, when the alarm sounds and well-armed and determined adversaries trample our values underfoot, is to do nothing at all.

Such was the fate in 1936 of the Popular Front in Spain, which was shamefully left to fall for fear of aggravating Hitler and Mussolini.

Such was the fate of Czechoslovakia in 1938.

It was the story of Berlin in 1953, Budapest in 1956, Prague in 1968, and Warsaw in 1981—the story behind the "of course we will do nothing" that, though uttered aloud only in the endgame by a member of French president François Mitterrand's cabinet, was from the outset the motto of a Europe immobilized by the mere idea of confronting the Red Army.

It was the story of the abandonment of Sarajevo to Serb militias between 1992 and 1995.

Except that here, in Kirkuk, there was no question of the Red Army.

Nor Mussolini's nor Hitler's.

Nor even the Serbian army, which passed, however erroneously, for one of the best of Europe.

There was only the Iraqi army.

The same army, now admittedly reequipped, that two years earlier had fled before the advance of the Islamic State.

The same force, devoid of any real military culture or patriotism, torn apart by sectarian rivalries between the Shiite majority and Sunni, Kurdish, and Christian minorities, that would have not stood for twenty-four hours after a Western warning shot.

It was before this army that the Europeans and the Americans had bowed.

Worse, it was their own arms—brand-new Abrams tanks delivered for the joint fight against ISIS—that the U.S. advisers and special forces on the ground allowed the Iraqis to turn against the Kurds.

And we witnessed the astonishing spectacle of the world's leading power consenting to the defeat and humiliation of its staunchest ally in the region. We saw the same President Trump, who had just declared Iran to be enemy number one in the complicated Middle East, voice no objection as Major General Qasem Soleimani, head of the

Quds Force, the elite unit of the Iranian Revolutionary Guards responsible for Iran's external operations, came and went, parading around the field of battle like a conqueror and posing for photographers. I myself reported, without drawing any correction or denial, the incredible scene in Kirkuk when, at around eight p.m. on October 15, the day of the decisive battle, another high-ranking Iranian officer screamed at a group of appalled Kurdish officers that "if you refuse to surrender, I will attack you here, here, and here," his finger jabbing at a map—this a few hundred meters from the airbase where American advisers were stationed.

The Kurds perceived this nonintervention as a terrifying enigma.

I will never forget the air of incredulity of Netchirvan Barzani, prime minister and nephew of the president, on the night in Erbil when, surrounded by his staff, he understood that Baghdad intended to follow through on its threats of a blockade. The confusion was general. Everyone occupied himself with something: one with a reassuring analysis of the overlapping interests that supposedly ensured that none of the protagonists could gain from escalation; another with a frantic Google search of the legal provisions relating to the airspace that Iraq was preparing to violate; still another with a phlegmatic disquisition on the eternal recurrence of the Kurdish curse and the prospect of having to take once again to the mountains that were, as people liked to say in Erbil, the only true friends of the Peshmerga. But Netchirvan Barzani's move was to call the allied capitals, one after the other, to alert them. And, as it dawned on him that there was no one at the other end of the line, he passed from shock to anger. A cold rage hardened his youthful and gentle features. No longer was he the modern leader, happy with the world, a cosmopolitan prince speaking Oxonian English, whose ambition, as I had gathered from our previous encounters, seemed to be to lead his people to prosperity on a Singaporean model. The tragic dimension of Kurdish destiny was catching up with him. His voice was dry and hard, his eyes dilated from the affront. There appeared on his face a look of controlled ferocity that I would have sworn was not native to him but rather came from one of those ancestors whose legacy of long-suffering heroism haunts every Kurd. Especially him, Netchirvan Barzani, whom all of us around the table knew to be the grandson of Mustafa Barzani, father of the Kurdish nation and of its school of resistance.

Nor will I forget how, the next morning, revisiting the former fronts at Gwer and in the Zartik Mountains, where the wind of emancipation had once briefly blown, I was surprised by the shock, the sad faces streaked with dried tears, and, above all, the anger—anger again—of people from whom I had parted just a few days ago as they exchanged their Kalashnikovs for ballots, raising index fingers stained with ink to show they had voted, aware of living through a historic moment. Now here they were again, realizing (late, because the Abrams tanks were rolling toward them) that they would have to take up their rifles again! When we reached Altun Kupri, thirty-six miles from Erbil, where the Iraqi army was already massing its forces, I was greeted with shouts of "America betrayed us" from a crowd of volunteers who had been busy building an improvised line of defense under a relentless sun relieved only intermittently by shade from the trees. "Why did America sell us out?" the fighters demanded. "For how much? And to whom?" But the clamor was lost in the penetrating rumble of pickup trucks being lined up to form a steel bulwark capable of slowing the advance of the Abrams tanks and then lost again in stanzas of a patriotic song, shouted out and whipped by the wind to leave only sonorous and somber repetitions of "Long live Kurdistan!" The ambient noise spared me from having to hazard an answer.

But what could I have said to those fighting voters riled up with rebelliousness?

Like them, I was thinking that this affair bore an unmistakable odor of betrayal.

Like them, I was shocked by the mixture of amateurism, fecklessness, and absence of vision of the U.S. and European administrations.

But the more time passed, the more I wondered if there was not something else in that black October, if we were not living through an event, a real one, one more loaded with meaning than it seemed, coming from farther back, headed farther into the future, and prefiguring, well beyond Kurdistan, a change of great magnitude that could not be explained simply by the treachery of great powers.

For such events do occur.

They creep up with the stealth of a wolf.

"On dove's feet," Nietzsche said.

The difference between doves and wolves is that the former bring peace whereas the latter enter cities only to spread fear and devastation: how true this was in Kirkuk!

But what they have in common is that we do not hear them coming.

In both cases, a third ear is needed to hear behind "the most silent voice" or the "still, small voice" (1 Kings 19:12) the echo of the soundless explosion, of the noiseless tumult, and, sometimes, of the shift of which they are the sign or the premonition.

Who grasped what was happening that day in 371 BCE when, in Leuctra, a desolate corner of the Greek region of Boeotia, the Sacred Battalion of Thebes cut to pieces the four hundred Spartiate Equals who were, like their Theban opponents and the Peshmerga, men who stood up in the face of death? Sparta still had unchallenged leaders, marble laws that were the admiration of the world, and another army, intact and undefeated. But the small battle of Leuctra sounded the death knell of its hegemony in Greece.

Who, thirty-three years later, at the Battle of Chaeronea, when all commentators, the Delphic oracle included, had eyes, ears, and words only for the destruction of the same Sacred Battalion by the cavalry of Philip II of Macedon, could discern that Athens was in fact the real target? That Athens was the true loser? That this was the beginning of the end for the empire of Solon, Miltiades, and Themistocles?

And the Battle of Pydna, on the border of Thessaly, which took place in 168 BCE? That was a lightning offensive (it took an hour) that might well have never taken place: a horse on the loose from the Roman lines, making to cross the river, provoked the first engagement and led King Perseus to believe that the enemy was on the move. Who, at the time, understood that it was the Macedonians' turn to suffer a historic defeat? To lose their grip and yield to the Romans? Who among the contemporaneous chroniclers grasped that Alexander's dream was fading away?

Some events seem rip-roaring but turn out to be mock occurrences.

Others, seemingly anodyne, are like delayed bolts of lightning, slow to strike and, once they do, slow to propagate before suddenly altering the course of history.

Anyway, that is what I felt.

When I boarded the last plane authorized to take off for Europe before the Iraqi embargo took effect and Kurdistan became the open-air prison that it remained for months, I was already convinced: we were in a situation akin to those I just cited. What was happening in Erbil reflected much more than President Trump permitting adjustments in the outlying provinces of the American empire. Something was at work that, with respect to America's relations with its allies, its partners, and itself, did not square with the old order and suggested the possibility of great shifts to come.

Back in Paris, I read up on who had said what in the debates within the UN Security Council about the "declaration" and the "resolution" that had been initiated by France and quickly emptied of substance through the interventions of China and Russia.

I saw a copy of the letter that the U.S. secretary of state, Rex Tillerson, had sent to President Barzani a few days before the September 25 referendum, in which Tillerson stated plainly that he was fully aware of the role the Peshmerga had played in ISIS's defeat and of the gratitude they were due as a result.

I had access to another memo from Tillerson, this one sent after the referendum to the Iraqi prime minister, Haider al-Abadi, asking him belatedly to cease fire, to accept the hand that the Kurds had extended, and to order the Shiite militias directed by Iran to leave Iraq.

In short, in reassembling the last pieces of the puzzle, I discovered something almost worse than nonintervention, blindness, and betrayal: when America decided to react, when it seemed to take the measure of the rout that it was inflicting on itself and finally spoke up, however timidly, its words fell flat and were ignored.

At that point, my conviction was set.

Fortune, as Polybius said, worked in the manner of a tragic playwright, improvising ups and downs, dramatic revelations, and reversals around one character's mediocrity (in this case an America First president indifferent to too-distant events), another character's tactical errors (here, the great but politically overconfident President Barzani), and yet another's hubris (the Iraqi prime minister's giddy discovery that his firmness in the face of the Kurds yielded him, in Baghdad, a degree of glory greater, at least for the moment, than what he had garnered from the collapse of the Islamic State). For anyone believing in universal history—that is, in the necessity of recounting the history of the world, as another Greek put it, "as if it were a single city"—it was clear that this featureless battle that concerned no one was, like Leuctra, Chaeronea, and Pydna, the occasion of a wide-ranging rebalancing of prestige and deterrent power in which a sapped America ceded its influence while its emboldened adversaries pushed their advantage and improvised an unprecedented redistribution of the systems of authority.

Iran on the move.

Turkey sensing that it need no longer hold back the

hatred it feels for the Kurdish people: a people almost as detestable and expendable in Turkish eyes as the Armenians.

A handful of Sunni states that, behind the example of Saudi Arabia, no longer hide their indifference for a small people who, although Muslim, are not Arab.

A power (Russia) and a superpower (China) that do whatever they can to stifle the Kurdish voice within the United Nations.

In short, five large or very large countries claiming new seats at the table of power—and doing so at the expense of the brave and noble Peshmerga.

One might object that what divides these five is greater than what unites them. Or that they exert no more influence over the course of the world than do others, such as Egypt or India. But this is the choice I make in this book. These are the five powers whose maneuvers I watched during those fearful days—five "kingdoms" I call them in reference to a Bible story about a "war of the empire against the five kings" that had always intrigued me but that, now, finally made sense. These are five kings who, in a word, shared the fact of having acted with respect to the Kurdish situation as if the American empire no longer mattered, as if we had entered a world without the United States—or, worse, as if we were returning to a pre-Columbian time when America did not yet exist.

Kurdistan as a mirror.

The battle of Kirkuk as a point at which disparate forces that had long been at work suddenly concentrated and refracted, tracing the contours of a new world order.

Historians will speak, I predict, of a Kirkuk moment— or more accurately of a Kirkuk epoch, because the word *epoch*, in Greek, signifies a halt, a suspension of the points of reference and the certitudes previously in force: a caesura, a spasm, and perhaps a new beginning.

A time is coming that is no longer the time that emerged from the death of communism, from the triumph of liberal values, and from the pronounced "end of history," an ending to which I never subscribed but that was beginning to take on a truly sinister face.

In Erbil, I felt the icy breath of the evil spirit of the world.

PART ONE

THE LATEST NEWS FROM THE EMPIRE

1

Hegel's Ghost

WHAT EXACTLY HAPPENED IN KIRKUK?

Was it an isolated and temporary deviation?

Can the blame be placed solely on an ignorant, inconsistent president?

I have lived in the United States. I have traveled the country extensively. Thirteen years ago, retracing the footsteps of Alexis de Tocqueville, I wrote a book about it. At the time, the country induced in this friendly observer a sense of vertigo. With this background, I have a simpler explanation. Unfortunately, it is also more worrisome.

The story begins a very long time ago.

And upon hearing it, one will understand that the position of the world's policeman, the protector of democratic values, or even the loyal ally of those I fault it for abandoning is not quite "natural" for the strange country that is America.

I remember the pages that Hegel devoted to the newborn United States in his *Lessons on the Philosophy of History*.

In substance, he wrote that its emergence was, of course, a major event.

Its appearance was part of the great linear movement from east to west that Hegel called universal history.

Because America lies at the far western end of that arc, it is there, Hegel insisted, that we can expect to witness the denouement of the inexorable plot in the course of which nations, through battles and conquests, contradictions faced and overcome, schisms, reconciliations, heroic acts, and negativities forsworn, are born, grow, and die.

With just one reservation—albeit a sizable one.

America was too big a country, almost empty, in fact—a country in which the land seemed like a sea and the people like sailors contending with waves of sand and rock.

It is a country whose spatial immensity imposed its law on a people of shepherds who roamed with their flocks to the sound of a cantilena that bore less resemblance to a country ballad than to a whaler's ditty.

It is, incidentally, the mirror image of the country that Melville would describe some years later in *Moby-Dick*, seeing in the rolling of the ocean's waves, below which panted the heart of the White Whale, an expanse not of water but of "long-drawn virgin vales," a cascade of "mild blue hill-sides," a "rolling prairie" where, like a "distant ship revealing only the tops of her masts" above the "high rolling waves," "the western emigrants' horses only show their erected ears, while their hidden bodies widely wade through the amazing verdure."

So that America, according to the philosopher of universal history (speaking like the first great bard of the American pastoral, though turning him on his head), is ultimately the site of a "perpetual motion," a restless "migration" with no final port, a place that presents the "impossibility of getting one's bearings."

Waves or grasses, it doesn't matter; stagecoaches surfing into valleys or birch bark canoes bobbing on the languor of an immense swell, they come to the same: the key point is that nothing lasting will ever be built there.

The same is true of the houses that Jean-Paul Sartre—revealing himself to be a Hegelian, or Melvillian, of stature—described in his great survey of America, published just after World War II, as always having a summary and almost uncouth aspect, set right on the ground, fragile, temporary, like a camp or caravan.

The same applies to the American hamlets about which so many travelers from Europe, accustomed to towns laden with history, rooted in dense soil, and with a discernible center, have wound up remarking: they make you think of interrupted visits or settlements living on borrowed time; you expect them at any moment to be dismantled, moved elsewhere, transformed; there they are—inhabited, bustling, alive, yet seemingly already on their way to their fate as a ghost town.

But the same applies, too, to the state that is, in proper Hegelian terms, the ultimate form of the house, the hamlet, the settlement, the city, the nation, and that is not able to find, any more than the rest of these, the conditions required for a stable foundation.

Hegel concluded that such an America was indeed the continuation of Europe; that it surely was, as one heard from all quarters, the "country of the future." One might even say, as Tocqueville would indeed later remark, that a "secret design of Providence" called it to hold "in its hands the destinies of half the world" and eventually to become the face of "the universal"—but only an *eventual* universal, one that is to come but is not yet mature, a universal still unsuitable, still insufficient, one that, for some time yet will embody only partly the uppercase universal of Mind.

In short, if one accepts the Hegelian term *predication* to signify how a historical power expresses itself and articulates its relation to the universal, if one consents to define "imperial" as the way in which some historical powers affect the rest of the planet and impose themselves on it, America's word can be only half-imperial because it is only half-predicative.

The American nation, as Hegel sees it, has its strength and its power.

It has waged victorious wars.

It will give birth to artists, writers, thinkers, whale hunters, heroes and monsters, slaves and masters who will battle each other without mercy.

But it lacks—and will continue for a long time to lack—something of that splendor, that self-confidence, that hubris that characterized, for example, the absolute power of seventeenth-century France or Renaissance Italy. It lacks, and will long lack, the imprimatur, the scar, of total authority.

I REMEMBER THE CIRCUMSTANCES IN WHICH I FIRST DISCOVERED those pages from Hegel and, for the sake of clarity, would like to return to that moment.

The time was shortly before May 1968.

I was in the first year of the preparatory course for the École Normale Supérieure at the Lycée Louis-le-Grand, in Paris, where I would skip the conventional philosophy courses in order to run over to the Collège de France to listen to the philosopher Jean Hyppolite, who was then in his last year of teaching. It was Hyppolite who gave the French language its first proper translation of Hegel and went on to provide a constant stream of learned commentary on Hegelianism.

I had also just met Benny Lévy, an Egyptian Jew unrelated to me, who was already a student at the École Normale and became my philosophy tutor by a circuitous route: My father had contacted the Hellenist Jean-Pierre Vernant, who, like himself, was a veteran of the Free French forces during World War II. Vernant in turn contacted Louis Althusser, his comrade in the Communist Party and my future professor, who led me to Benny. At the time, Benny Lévy was the charismatic leader of the most radical Maoist group in France. Only a quarter of a century later would he become a master of Orthodox Judaism. The strangely predestined nature of this chain of friendship still amazes me fifty years later.

One day, sitting in a café near the Collège de France with two friends and Benny, who was still assembling the components of a Maoism that he wished to be as philosophically exemplary as it was exemplarily radical, I found myself face-to-face with Jean Hyppolite, the legendary professor who, in a gravelly voice coarsened by smoking, was endeavoring, text in hand, to tell us the story of America according to Hegel, while miming, with the gestures of an orchestra conductor, the thesis, antithesis, and synthesis of Hegel's and Marx's dialectics.

This was a time, it must be remembered, when the name of this austere scholar, Jean Hyppolite, was engraved alongside those of scholars of similar mettle on the pediment of the pantheon of thinkers most highly regarded by radical young minds.

It was an odd time when, to paraphrase a French poet, or rather two, we were at once unreasonable and highly prone to ratiocination, rebellious and logical—and when the more severe the mathematics, the more inflexible the science, the more doggedly and scientifically our professors stalked the strict and naked truth, the more they seemed suitable (by virtue of a reversal that had little to do with dialectics) for mobilization into the little army of those who were going to help us break the history of the world in two.

For the young people we were, there was in that a paradoxical episteme in which rigor was related to rebellion; in which the canons of knowledge seemed like guarantors of the desire for revolution; and in which the most abstract and ethereal analyses, those most detached from immediate political issues, appeared under a halo of metaphorical meaning meant as a secret code for the cognoscenti—that is, for us. Behind Louis Althusser's "epistemological break," we discerned proletarian revolution. Under the pavement of Foucault's *Madness and Civilization* lay the ash-strewn shore, littered with the nameless and unconfessed, that we dreamt of finding. And when Jean Hyppolite, with his strong jaw and massive features in constant movement (causing him to resemble an anxious Jean Gabin), spoke to us of the "semi-predicative" America according to Hegel, when he described America's embarrassed empire and its discomfort with predication, we could only take him at his word and, in his words, hear a denunciation of the Trotskyites and other leftist sects with which we were competing, who believed, as do the populist movements of today, in a tentacled, diabolical, all-powerful American imperialism responsible for all of the world's problems. Not us.

It is always useful to remember the path that truths had to take to reach the wall of our convictions and find a chink in which to lodge.

In our case, this is how the knot was tied, through a dialogue of auditors with a Jean Hyppolite who could not have cared less about the fierce determination of the Latin Quarter's Maoists to stand like a revolutionary aristocracy against the buskers of the Communist International but who inspired in us such great respect that his word was gold.

I am proud to say that, since that moment, I have never engaged in the sin against sense that is anti-Americanism.

Never, since that day, have I thought that the United States was a force of evil busy building an empire of the type that all the true colonial powers built before and after it.

There is, of course, the founding crime of the extermination of the American Indian, but that was taken to heart and has been duly mourned—in the process, the famous "political correctness" that, in other settings, has caused so much damage found one of its noblest applications.

Likewise, there is the bloody shadow cast for so long by the smug practice of slavery—but then came Lincoln's

Emancipation Proclamation, Rosa Parks, Martin Luther King, and Barack Obama.

And the fact is that, if there is a trap into which I have never fallen (from the time of the demonstrations against the Vietnam War, where I got my political education, right up to the election of Donald Trump, which appalled me as an admirer of America), it is the hysterical condemnation, the demonization, the malignant hypostasis of an "inner" and "ontological" America—the very concept of which has always struck me as a sure sign of the worst kind of thinking.

Imagine a scale capable of weighing the good and the bad that people do. On such a scale, Hiroshima; the support given to dictatorships in Brazil, Chile, and the rest of Latin America; the napalm used in Vietnam; and, now, "America First." But don't they weigh less than the role of the United States in the two world wars? Its two rescues of Europe? Its strong, constant, and ultimately victorious stand against various forms of communism? Its punishment of the butchers of the Bosnian War? The liberation of Kosovo? The war against the Taliban in Afghanistan? The worldwide fight against radical Islam, up to and excluding the treatment of Kurdistan?

But it is not only that, on balance, the United States seems to have done more good than harm. It is that Hyppolite's idea impressed me from a philosophical perspective and struck me as a valid proposition in the realm of mind and truth. How amazed I was when I saw that this same idea was embraced by André Malraux (one of my masters of life even more than of thought) when he declared, in a letter to the president of the United States, Richard Nixon, written a few weeks after Malraux's scheduled departure for Bangladesh in 1971: "The United States is the first country to have become the most powerful in the world without having sought it. Alexander wanted to be Alexander, Caesar wanted to be Caesar, but you never wanted to be masters of the world."

André Malraux was disapproving.

Specifically, he disapproved that Richard Nixon's America, which was allied with Pakistan, would not use force to stop the massacre of the Bengalis.

He found it unacceptable "that the country of the Declaration of Independence should crush the wretched as they fight for their own independence."

Hyppolite, by contrast, was not judging but rather simply observing.

Specifically, he observed that America was what it was: modest, reluctant to impose itself, and, by virtue of a law that proceeded from the singular way it had come into the adventure of being and spirit, condemned to wield semi-predicative power.

But here, in the conjunction of Malraux and Hyppolite, was one of those alignments of the stars that decide the fate of a young man.

In the end, the proposition, validated by a master of truth *and* by a professor of courage, gained the force of law.

The United States is a power, but one that never entirely sought empire's glory.

It is an empire, if you will, but a recalcitrant one, whose nobility has always been to balk at imperialism.

All right, it has sometimes looked like an imperialistic empire—but a clumsy, awkward one, sometimes too heavy-handed, at other times too quick on the draw.

Imperialistic, yes, but often of necessity, as when no one else was left to confront the Nazis and their allies—and even then immature, adolescent: Didn't the Americans confess as much when, succumbing to an unbelievable Freudian slip, they named the Hiroshima bomb "Little Boy"?

It is an empire, in other words, that is an exception to the unabashed imperiousness, punctuated by wars of conquest, that was the common principle of the succession of empires according to Polybius (Persia, Sparta, Macedonia, Rome) and the prophet Daniel (who added Babylonia).

So it cannot be ruled out that, with its present retreat, America is returning to a state that, on balance, it finds more natural than the position of world fireman that it has occupied for a little less than a century.

Some may find this reassuring.

Others—friends of America and of the values for which it stands—find it heartbreaking and are appalled to see the country take stances like the one it took during the

Bangladesh war or, more recently, during the battle of Kirkuk and the war in Kurdistan.

But, once again, we are dealing with a law that is both metaphysical and political.

And its secret lies in Hegel more than in the caprices, the character, and the tragic errors of Donald Trump.

2

How the Word Came to America

But how did things really happen?

How did this immature, awkward, semi-predicative imperial vocation fall onto the shoulders of the Americans, and how did it fall so squarely that, until lately, it seemed to define them?

The truth is that they assumed it only recently, a century and a half after Hegel's assessment. But, even then, it was by default and, again, reluctantly. And that is the essential message of the chain of events that begins with the end of World War II and over which I must linger for a moment.

In ordinary wars, both sides would pretend that they had won.

In *Candide*, Voltaire gives us the scene at the end of the conflict between the Bulgares and the Abares, when "the two kings were having Te Deums sung, each in his own camp."

But World War II was not an ordinary war.

It was a long war, one that began in 1914 and went on for thirty-one years.

It was one of those rare wars that, since Erich Ludendorff's 1935 essay, we have called "total wars."

And it was a war in which one of the belligerents committed unprecedented crimes that wounded humanity to its core.

After such a war, the quarrel between the Abares and the Bulgares is no longer relevant.

In such a war, one actor, and one only, wins—unequivocally and irrefutably.

And winning, then, means more than crushing the enemy, preventing him from rearming, or occupying his territory. It means, once the guns are stilled and the vanquished are reduced to silence, assuming the right to set the rhetoric to be used in the drafting of the treaties and to define the political and legal models upon which national and international institutions would be built. A victorious nation is one that, because its bloodied battalions and its bombs gave rise to the new order of things, because its military police have begun to protect the fragile peace on yesterday's fields of battle, assumes the upper hand in administering not only the soil but also the symbols that will repopulate the world as it reemerges from the ruins.

The victorious nation objectifies its victory by unleashing on the historical moment not only its soldiers but also its language—that is, its experience of the world.

It has not completely won until it has formulated a new meaning that will impose its authority on humanity.

And that new meaning is at first as dazzling as a scorching sun, as imperious as a spring torrent, before gradually becoming diffuse and mild, ample and undisputed, like autumnal wisdom.

So what exactly occurred within the georhetoric of the global moment marked by the defeat of Nazism?

What language was best suited, on May 8, 1945, to the task of both revealing and healing the wounds, of taking charge of things, of finding meaning in a world so totally disoriented?

It obviously could not be the language of Germany, which, regardless of its secular affinities with the idiom of thinkers and poets, regardless of the political, economic, and financial power that it would regain soon enough, was barred for a very long time as a source of historical narrative and meaning.

It could not be a language of Asia, given how irretrievably compromised Japan was and how the terrible communist misadventure gathering steam in China, an episode that would soon isolate the country, was taking it out of play and delaying the onset of its present imperial ambitions.

It might have been the language of France, a member of the winning side that has at times in its history dreamed of holding imperial authority and proffering its tongue as a plausible pretender to the title of universal language. It missed out by a hair. It would not have taken much (Quebec is the proof) for the North American continent, like the western part of Russia, Brazil, and Europe as a whole, to have spoken a little or a lot of French—perhaps even enthusiastically.

It was not to be. A legend—the legend of the Resistance—was not enough to erase the memory of Europe's leading army crushed in a matter of five weeks along the Meuse and in the Ardennes.

But even if that had not been the case—even if the French army had held, even if Vichy had not existed, even if General Charles de Gaulle's Free French forces had been France and had fought shoulder to shoulder with the Allies for five long years, even if this, even if that, there was in France's very language and in the image of the world that it offered to its speakers something that had become resistant to the idea of global authority.

Was it the decline of Catholicism and its defining principle?

Was it France's passage into the second phase of the history of a nation, that of disillusion, of the Grail forever lost? "We have to reinvent a national narrative," people say. But they know that what they are being exhorted to reinvent is just a narrative and that, even if they returned to believing it, it would be by agreement rather than faith.

Or was it something deeper, something having to do with the actual history of the French mind and the shared experience that a common language provides?

I look back on the France of the preceding half century.

I reflect on the prodigious brilliance of the septet of Mallarmé, Debussy, Monet, Rimbaud, Bergson, Ravel, and, most of all, Marcel Proust.

I see how one of the septet was able to make light out of nothing, another to turn the nothingness of light into colors, yet another to create shape, substance, and even life from the next to nothing that is the scent of a lilac or the light opacity of fog.

I hear the echo of the voice of Proust, who distilled and orchestrated the others of the group—Proust the impressionist genius, Proust the other painter of water lilies who sets his blooms in ponds of words formed by the Vivonne River. And then there are his lunar arpeggios, the sobs that sound like sarcasm, the listless drops from Hubert Robert's streams of water glimpsed in the gardens of the Duchess of Guermantes.

It is a moment of dazzling brilliance.

A pinnacle of French greatness that will last and last.

But that greatness—subtle, sparkling, incandescent— was of another sort than its earlier incarnation, which paired so well with the building of a French empire.

Yes, the new wave of greatness beckoned—but to a voyage to Kythera, not for an adventure intended to impose meaning.

And when the time came for the decisive confrontation, for a pronouncement on how the world would have to be if it was to be inhabited by the survivors of the carnage, when the other empire's time came, the virtuous empire, the one that gathers the victors around a table and says to the rest of the world, "Hear me, I am speaking," the best of the French language was, so to speak, elsewhere.

Yes, there was Charles de Gaulle, a speaker of great style who inhabited his own name, the name of France, and the names and nouns of a French language stretched to the breaking point.

But amid how many divisions?

Despite his personal ascendency, who was there to heed his claim of French legitimacy?

And if, in the interlingual arbitrage into which the settlement of such a war resolves, de Gaulle's language managed to achieve official status at the United Nations, it was an extremely close call, a victory won on the strength of a boldness and that, looking back, leaves one speechless.

When a language says, "I know," and then goes on to

whisper, "there is nothing to know," when its best practitioners are master doubters, disabusers, disillusionists, disenchanters, and negators (in the noble sense of the word), that language can no longer be the voice of a doctrine of positivity. It has been transformed into something else. It is no longer cut out for imperium.

THE LANGUAGE OF THE VICTORY MIGHT HAVE BEEN RUSSIAN.

For the Soviet Union, too, was in the victors' camp.

And all historians know that, without the Soviet Union and its sacrifices, without its twenty-five million war dead (counting both civilian and military deaths), fully half of the total deaths in the war, without the tactical and strategic brilliance of its generals, Nazism would not have been defeated.

But it's not enough to be a victor.

The victory I have in mind here, the kind that allows the victor to universalize a story and a meaning, must be moral as well as military.

And two reasons explain why the Soviet Union could not have won that victory and why, moreover, it did not really seek it.

The first is related to its early collusion with the enemy. How can you be awarded the trophy for anti-Nazism when you began by sealing a pact with Hitler? When you believed so strongly in this pact that you refused to recognize its annulment until the very last minute? And when neither the war that eventually erupted, nor the horrifying blood-bath that it inflicted on your people, nor the fight to the death of two rival titans, Hitler and Stalin, cannot suppress the feeling of an unspoken but irrevocable complicity between the proletarian spirit of Moscow and the "prole-taryan" spirit of Berlin?

But there is a second and weightier reason why the Soviet Union never seriously aspired to the intellectual and moral leadership of the post–World War II world, notwith-standing the Cassandras who, in the wake of the suppres-sion of the 1953 workers' revolts in Berlin, envisioned tanks rolling up to the gates of Paris.

In fact, the Soviet Union made a choice.

It is a choice that may appear at odds with the aggres-sive (to say the least) turn that its foreign policy took for fifty years—from Cuba to Afghanistan, from the Prague coup to all the terrible plots carried out against its former allies in the anti-Nazi coalition.

But in the perspective adopted here, in the not exactly *geopolitical* but, to borrow from the Scottish writer Ken-neth White, *geopoetic* order in which the fate of nations is written, it seems that it was indeed a choice—one appro-priate, moreover, to the circumscribed strengths of its lead-ers and to the ample imagination of its greatest writers.

That choice was for the land.

It was to take the measure—or, more precisely, the immeasurability—of the vast Russian landmass, and of the bordering lands that it converted into satellites for the sake of the "living space" it claimed to require.

So that, at the moment when the English-speaking world, and the Americans in particular, set out to conquer sky and sea, as they redoubled their efforts to build towers that pierced the clouds and began the process of flooding the planet with their algorithms and waves, the Russians were sinking their feet and hands into the mud; they immersed themselves in a continent of steppe, turf, and ice that seems never to reach the sea, or, when it does, reaches an inner sea, one domesticated and then abandoned, like the Aral Sea, left to revert to its true state of poisoned land. They won the war—yes, they did—but, for them, winning meant swallowing up space and getting drunk on tellurism; against the glass towers, the airy immateriality of computation and exchange, against the strength in numbers that would make New York the financial capital and, later, Silicon Valley the digital capital of the planet, the Soviets placed a different kind of strength: the bulky, ponderous, pachydermic weight of matter.

While at it, the Soviet Union swallowed half of Europe; but that was because it saw Eastern and Central Europe as the extension of its territory, the fringe of the glacier.

Steppes, taigas, tundras, Polish forests, Romanian mountains, Hungarian countryside, Danubian bridges, and, why not, peoples, cities, churches, artworks, treasures of history and memory: it is all good, all fair game, but only as long as it can be converted into something truly real and measurable in miles and tons, optionally stocked with some human clay and spiced up with a little culture.

It is only in Tolstoy (and perhaps Charles Péguy) that you find people crying over a sheaf of wheat and burying it in a coffin.

It is only in Russia (and maybe in France, though in a different sense) that wheat is money, really and truly money. Americans also have wheat, of course, but you do not find them worshipping it! They long ago reduced it to prices, reserves, futures, and trend lines.

Thus spoke Russia: brutally, cynically, using people as pawns in a war that had to remain, indeed, a cold war.

And so went the Russian nation, competing with the language of the empire or aping it, but never seriously believing that its International would extend to the entire human race.

AMERICA WAS ALL THAT WAS LEFT.

More precisely, what was left in 1945 was the Anglo-American bloc that the European Far Right, for decades, referred to as "Anglamerica," whose hand (usually with help from Jews and Freemasons) it claimed to see behind the dark plots that made up the underside of contemporary history.

What was left was that two-headed eagle (London,

New York) that Martin Heidegger immediately concluded was the consummate metaphysical adversary—much more so than the Soviet bear, which he saw as a caricature of national socialism.

What was left was that "democratic empire"—Heidegger often termed it "English Bolshevism"—that the German "imperial dictatorship" had been sent to defeat in order to restore, in the nick of time, humanity's "lost confidence in Being."

Except that the democratic empire won.

And it won, of course, by managing to overcome enemy armies, by dropping Little Boy on Hiroshima, and by assigning GIs to patrol the capitals of the defeated Axis; but, even more certainly, it won by imposing on the rest of the world its law, its vision, its language, and, in Heideggerese, the modality of its relation to Being.

So it came to be that, in the realm of law, we had the Nuremberg Trials, made possible by the anglicization of the concepts of genocide and crimes against humanity invented by two Central Europeans from L'viv—Raphael Lemkin and Hersch Lauterpacht—who took refuge in the United States and Great Britain, respectively.

So it came to be that, in the realm of institutions, we had the United Nations charter, after a group of neo-Wilsonians, feeling nostalgic about a British Empire whose hour they knew had passed, gathered in San Francisco to internationalize the concept of the "open society": Proposed by Karl Popper at the outset of the hostilities, that concept contrasted the universality of human rights with the determinism of tribal, magical, and authoritarian societies; and the UN charter, though regularly trampled and betrayed in the succeeding years, represented a hope for humanity.

America did something similar when it globalized Adam Smith's intuition about the efficiency, virtue, and civilizing force of a market that, for the first time in history, broke away from the system of pillage and spoils and, from its towers, laid out a new kind of space, one exempt from the force of gravity and not bound by frontiers or time—a sort of noumenal space floating above the material world and its phenomenal encumbrances: in this new space, people were able to exchange infinite quantities of goods and services from any point in the cosmos and in less time than it takes to make up your mind.

The absolute sign of this victory, its last installment and defining moment, was the admission into that space of post-Stalinist Russia after decades of what seemed like fierce resistance but was revealed in retrospect to be no more than a rearguard action.

When the last general secretary of the Communist Party of the Soviet Union deplaned onto the tarmac bearing the tame American sobriquet of "Gorby," when he launched a program of *glasnost* (which in Russian means "airing of debates" or "freedom of expression and opinion," but which the world, as one, immediately, and with no objection from anyone, came to translate as the quint-essentially American "openness" or "transparency"), and when an intellectual named Francis Fukuyama rendered into the language of Leo Strauss and Allan Bloom the Hegelian prophecy of history reaching its culmination, putting a full stop at the end of its ideological evolution and coming more or less willingly to attention before the values of democracy, liberty, and law (even in the eastern regions that only yesterday seemed to be resisting)—well, when this happened, the matter was settled and the United States won, decisively and conclusively.

But hold on.

It won by default.

Its final victory, the one against communism, came without combat and with hardly anyone predicting it.

And as for the initial victory, the one that launched the whole story and that, contrary to Heidegger's prophecy, made the American spirit the savior of a continent that, because of Nazism, had very nearly succeeded in committing suicide a second time, it must be remembered that this victory was possible only because a patrician by the name of Franklin Delano Roosevelt had used all his strength, character, and cleverness to defeat American isolationism. In so doing, Roosevelt had to overcome the first America First movement, which in 1940, lest we forget, was a dominant strain of the country's foreign policy. Roosevelt personally forced a resistant America to fabricate an empire.

To borrow the phrase not of André Malraux, but of another French novelist, Paul Morand, Americans were "involuntary Romans."

This is the setting.

Moving from miracles into the real world and from geopoetics to political order, this is the true story of the late-arriving, fragile, and initially indecisive Pax Americana that I watched unravel in Kirkuk.

— *3* —

Lest I Forget You,
Jerusalem, Aeneas, Virgil

BUT THAT'S NOT ALL.

A part of the political, mythological, and symbolic inheritance of the United States predisposed it, when the time came, to an imperial predication, however recalcitrant.

And at least two themes in its geopoetical armamentarium were compatible with saving Europe and, later, assuming the position of a great, liberal power ready to defend the values of freedom, more or less, all over the world.

But what is happening now, the quietly decisive and almost invisible event that is profoundly changing things, is that these two themes are losing their power.

———

THE FIRST WAS THE APPEAL OF JERUSALEM.

The pilgrim fathers, arriving on the far shore of the Atlantic, were determined to be a new Chosen People in a new Promised Land.

The idea of America was incomprehensible without the millenarian notion of a new land of milk and honey to which one might go and build a Jerusalem on earth without waiting for the end of days, skipping the steps set out in the Old Testament and the Gospels.

And that was the meaning of the famous "exceptionalism" formulated by John Winthrop, in the spring of 1630, during the voyage that took him from the Old World to the New. We have a special pact with the Lord, Winthrop told his flock. We will be a model of charity and Christian virtue. We will be the "city upon a hill" proclaimed in Jesus's Sermon on the Mount.

It is easy to see what is strange, from a strictly theological perspective, in this promise.

We know that for most Judeo-Christians, it is heresy to shove aside the order of things and purport to erect, right here, right now, without waiting for the resurrection, a new Jerusalem of jasper, sapphire, and chalcedony.

And we also know that it is possible to give an isolationist reading to this heresy upon which the United States was built: Is not the main purpose of Manifest Destiny to manifest itself? Is not the first job of a city on a hill to be seen, simply seen, visible and offered up for the admiration of the nations of the world? And is it not enough for the New Jerusalem to be a jewel, blazing with a thousand fires, dazzling the world with its incandescent beauty?

But there is another possible reading to give to this credo.

In the actual history of the sects and churches that made up the United States of America, no less strong than this first reading has been the temptation to encourage the world to move from admiration to adhesion, from amazement to imitation, and, when the movement was not rapid enough, when distant lands were slow to adopt the canons of the sublime city, to give them a little shove in the right direction.

To put it plainly, I think that Woodrow Wilson's decision to go to war against Germany in 1917, Franklin Roosevelt's resolution to join the battle against fascism in 1941, and, moving into caricatural mode, George W. Bush's contorted and ill-fated operation to bring down Saddam Hussein's dictatorship in Iraq in 2003, all drew from the same well.

The paradigm was the same: a belief in the exceptional role of an American nation called upon to pick up the torch that had fallen from the fragile hands of the prophets and apostles of the City of God; and the mission was to carry that torch into dark lands.

———

THE SECOND THEME IS THE VIRGILIAN DREAM.

Why Virgilian?

Because Virgil is the poet who, in *The Aeneid*, recounts how Rome was founded by a survivor of the burning city of Troy.

Because it is he who told us that the colossal Roman Empire had its origins in the odyssey of a single man, Aeneas, who took off with the guardian deities of defeated Troy and arrived, several years and several seas later, in the terra incognita of Italy.

And because that was the other idea lodged in the heads of the first pioneers when they set off for America: to flee Amsterdam, Paris, London, or Plymouth, those new Troys consumed by the fire of persecution and tyranny; to take a moment, before boarding the boat, to capture the flickering flames of the guardian deities of the cities of Europe (those deities being the spirit of tolerance, a predilection for the common good and for law, and the idea of freedom); and, at the end of a long and exhausting voyage during which they, too, were the playthings of higher powers, were led to gates of hell, and were tempted a thousand times to fall into discouragement and to give up, those pioneers found, as Aeneas and his companions had found on the shores of Latium, a "virgin" soil on which to release their Lares, Manes, Penates, and other household divinities whom they had washed in the deep waters of the new Mediterranean that was the Atlantic Ocean.

We know that Thomas Jefferson was a fervent reader

of Virgil and that fidelity to the European origins of the country he helped to found was one of the reasons that led him, in 1793, to call for active support for the French Revolution, in opposition to the president he served, George Washington.

We know that *The Aeneid* was bedside reading for great Latinists like the Puritan clergyman Cotton Mather; the poet Samuel Low, whose ode lauded the ratification of the U.S. Constitution; the group of Boston citizens who urged the king of England to adopt a better pastoral policy; Charles Thomson, the secretary of the Continental Congress and designer of the Great Seal of the United States; and, much later, the journalist John O'Sullivan, opponent of the death penalty, precocious feminist, and inventor (in sympathy with the best of Italic and, by extension, European heritage) of the concept of Manifest Destiny.

One has only to inspect the dollar bill to find not just one but three quotations from Virgil. First, on the back, at left, circling the truncated pyramid capped with the eye of Providence and subtitled, in Roman numerals, with the date of the Declaration of Independence, are the words *novus ordo seclorum*: taken from the fourth eclogue of the *Bucolics*, these words announce "a new order of the ages." Above that, we find *annuit cœptis*, which means "favor our undertakings": it's a free adaptation of a verse from the *Georgics* in which the poet implores the divinity not to abandon him. And finally, at right, held in the beak of the eagle that was also a symbol of Rome, we have a banner with the famous phrase "E pluribus unum" that also appears on the Great Seal, which conveys patriotic "unity" from a "plurality" of origins: "E pluribus unum" is an adaptation of a verse from *Moretum*, another bucolic that was believed, at the time, to have been written by Virgil.

The mission of these early Americans is clear.

It is to express, extend, and expand upon Virgil and *The Aeneid*.

It is to prolong, still farther west, the great adventure that began in Troy and continued with the founding of Alba Longa and then Rome, before finding its provisional fulfillment on the shores of New England.

The references, not just to Latin but specifically to Virgil's Latin, signify an unbreakable tie to Europe as a land of ruins both moral and material, a land that one has left behind without regret while feeling certain of having saved the best part and firmly intending to bring it back to life, as Aeneas did.

And the nostalgia for Europe, the regret converted into resolution, the metaphysical decision to replay the invention of Europe is the second well from which the descendants of the Pilgrims and the Puritans drew in 1917 and again in 1941, when they retraced their steps, made the founding trip in reverse, and undertook to save the continent whence they had come.

A strict reader of the Bible will not fail to observe that it is not easy to be faithful simultaneously to Jerusalem and to Rome.

And such a reader might even point out that the holy city, the new Jerusalem come "down from God out of heaven," is the opposite, term for term, of the blood-drunk whore from Revelation whose name is Babylon, which is another name for Edom, and thus for Rome, and thus for Europe.

Be that as it may.

America, when she embarks on imperial predication, even halfheartedly, is Jerusalem plus Rome.

Generous America, friend of democracy abroad as well as at home, is Isaiah plus Virgil.

It is—was—necessary to combine these two reasons so that the American dream could present itself as a dream for all, one with universal pretensions, even if this was only half true.

I TURN NOW TO TODAY'S AMERICA, THE ONE THAT FAILED IN Kirkuk.

And I have to say that these two pillars, which weathered the centuries well, are now, for the first time, cracking and giving way.

On the Virgilian side, we can date the reversal from the day in 1956 that the U.S. Congress voted to replace "E pluribus unum," which had always been the country's motto, with the less bucolic "In God we trust."

We might date it from the death of the one and only Roman Catholic president that America ever elected—in other words, from the cyclonic, everlasting blow that was the assassination of John Fitzgerald Kennedy.

Closer to the present day, we can date it from the moment when the God that the descendants of the founders of America were asked to believe in became a national, naturalized American God, one literally made in the U.S.A.—the moment when, in other words, the neo-evangelistic mega-churches became the country's leading religion. America continues, of course, to be home to Jewish communities still living in the unchanging time of Rashi and Rosenzweig. It remains the homeland of traditional Episcopalians, Lutherans, Methodists, and Presbyterians. There is a large and powerful contingent of Catholics, all the more attached to Roman dogma and the apostolic succession for being surrounded by neo-Protestantism. But in this country that is so ready to believe, that made faith a civic imperative, and where it is hard to distinguish religious from political pastoral work, many U.S. religious leaders now seem to want to say to the world: yes, Europe produced Martin Luther; Rome venerated the Virgin Mary; and yes, on the edge of all that, there was an Egyptian Jew named Moses and a Nazarene Jew named Jesus; but America is God's country; across what had been a new England but is now America, we built churches—Baptist, Pentecostal, evangelical—that are our national churches rooted in our heads and in our territory; so farewell, friends, long and distant cousins in Christianity; we are no longer the farm team, minor league Anglicans whose credo consisted of being more European than the Europeans; good-bye to all that.

And one can date it, naturally, from the moments when the last two presidents of the United States, Barack Obama and Donald Trump, matched their actions to the prevailing discourse and let it be known that Europe was no longer a priority for the United States.

In Trump's case, the message was delivered with the vulgarity for which he is known. It came with his mad exit from the Paris climate accord in 2017. With his advice to Germany to rely on its own strengths—namely its trade surpluses—to assure its own defense. And with all the statements early in his term that caused his erstwhile allies to wonder how the president of America First would respond if a major crisis led NATO to invoke Article 5 of the North Atlantic Treaty. Would Trump still consider an "armed attack" occurring in Europe as an attack on the United States? Would he rise to the defense of the country or countries attacked? Or would he deem that the security of the Baltic states, Poland, or the Czech Republic was no longer a priority for him?

On July 15, 2018, at the end of a weeklong tour of Europe and on the eve of a meeting with Vladimir Putin in which he would appear shockingly weak and submissive, he let it all hang out: not only was Europe the "socialist" continent that he had scourged in 2011; not only was it the vast market whose common currency he declared in 2013 to have been created to "harm the United States";

not only was it the inconvenient rival whose incipient dismemberment he celebrated on the occasion of the Brexit vote in 2016—no, by July 15, 2018, in a mind-blowing interview with CBS News, he went so far as to say that Europe was nothing less than "the enemy of the United States"! The page was turned. Virgil's thread was broken.

But a similar message had been conveyed, albeit with more ceremony and much more style and intelligence, over the eight preceding years. Remember when the dashing, elegant, and brilliant Barack Obama, at the start of his first term, declined to attend an important European summit. When the same Obama appeared to allow the National Security Agency to tap the personal cell phone of Chancellor Angela Merkel and, when word got out, played down the offense. When he skipped the twenty-fifth anniversary of the fall of the Berlin Wall in favor of an Asian tour and then, two months later, begged off from the demonstration of solidarity for the victims of the attacks in Paris against *Charlie Hebdo* and the kosher market with the flimsy excuse of an "overloaded schedule." When he acted as if his fondest vision was to see a Silicon Valley on Mount Fuji and implied that America's future lay to the west, still farther west, without realizing that, the earth being round, the distant west was back in the Far East. And when he made it known that he wanted his two terms to be known for the tilt toward Asia, for putting relations with Russia back on an even keel, and for the nuclear deal with Iran.

By the time he came to Berlin late in his second term to speak on the importance of Europe, he no doubt wanted to repair his mistake. But the gesture had the feel of a last-minute correction or of an earnest student not wanting to leave any box unchecked. And the impressions that will last are that Obama said with a smile what Trump says with a scowl; that Obama acted as if the sun were shining while Trump grumbles about the weather; that Obama was all sweetness and light whereas Trump thunders about days of wrath; and that, with respect to Europe's importance to the United States, the two presidents' similarities outweigh their differences.

Not to mention the other abandonment of Europe—and of France in particular—that came at the end of August 2013 when Obama did a U-turn on the question of Bashar al-Assad's use of chemical weapons in Syria. He laid down a "red line." He threatened dire consequences if that line were crossed. And then, when it was crossed, he did an about-face and froze, leaving French president François Hollande, his planes ready to take off, to sort things out on his own. That will go down as a bad day in the history of transatlantic relations—and as a turning point in the deterioration of American deterrence. And for that, alas, we have Obama to thank, not Trump.

So much for America conceived as the evening land.

Pull the curtains on this "Levant," this sunrise, that shone far in the east, and whose completion and fulfillment were its deep vocation.

Good-bye Europe of ancient parapets; good-bye Caesar, Julius and Augustus, emperors of West and East; good-bye *Georgics, Bucolics, Aeneid*; good-bye Latin meter and Roman verse, which were the bywords of the inventors of America, their language of heart and mind, the "sacred yeast" of America, much as Aeneas and Priam were Rome's "holy seed" in Dante's *Inferno.*

For the first time in its history, America springs from nothing but itself.

For the first time, it is cutting the dimly glowing thread that it had heretofore maintained between itself and what Hegel had called "old Europe."

And Trump, who saw himself as Caesar, instead resembles Romulus Augustulus, Rome's last emperor, a dreary, feebleminded character who has always reminded me of the fat little Hapsburg in Fellini's *And the Ship Sails On* and whose name is such a boon for a writer: Romulus, the name borne by Rome's founder, as well as by the man who dug its grave; and Augustulus, the august name synonymous with classical splendor disfigured by the diminutive suffix that derides the greatness of which Virgil sang the praises. In real life, Romulus Augustulus was a cruel and ridiculous child-king. In the "nonhistorical comedy in four acts" that Friedrich Dürrenmatt devoted to him, he is a sovereign of whom it is hard to know whether he is criminal ("I was left with no other possibility," he says, "other than to become emperor myself in order to be able to liquidate the empire") or senile (for spending his days in his henhouse clucking, which is not far from tweeting, in unison with his fowl). In the end, he turned his empire over without a fight to the German prince, Odoacer, before beginning a quiet retirement. Could that be Mr. Trump's plan? Could that be a clue to his strange behavior before the Odoacers of our time—Putin for one, or any of the illiberal dictators who, from every corner of the world, challenge and often trample the values of freedom, tolerance, and democracy that have been America's credo from its beginnings?

WITH RESPECT TO JERUSALEM, THE QUESTION APPEARS TO BE more complex.

First because the evangelical Christian right in the United States insists that the return of all the world's Jews to Jerusalem is a necessary precursor of Jesus's return to earth.

And next because President Trump, in fulfillment of a promise made to the Christian right during the campaign, made the historic decision to move the American embassy in Israel to the Holy City.

But this move, which was welcomed by many Jews and friends of Israel as a courageous gesture that simply put reality straight with the law, should be viewed in a broader context for at least three reasons.

Reason one is that this neo-evangelical, anti-European form of Zionism has very little in common with Israel's importance to the architects of American exceptionalism and Manifest Destiny. It is a form of Zionism that is a stranger to humanist, liberal values; that considers Jews as bit players in a spectacle that concerns them only indirectly; and that is prepared, to get where it wants to go, to push aside the Jews, body and soul. In this current of thought, the Jewish people's wholesale return to the Holy Land is considered a prelude to their conversion. And from this point of view, there is nothing very surprising in the fact that among the guests of honor invited to bless the new embassy were a pair of strange evangelical pastors, John Hagee and Robert Jeffress. Hagee, who founded an organization known as Christians United for Israel in 2006, has asserted, among other enormities, that Adolf Hitler was partly of Jewish origin and that the Holocaust was, despite its horror, God's plan. As for Jeffress, who had delivered the sermon at the service marking Donald Trump's arrival at the White House, he is the same man who, in 2008, declared that Judaism leads straight to hell, and then, in 2010, opined that "you can't be saved being a Jew," citing as his source for this certitude "the three greatest Jews in the New Testament: Peter, Paul, and Jesus Christ."

Reason two is that there is a world of difference between the two things. On one side, a political decision, that is to say, the decision of a politician who is visibly ignorant of the laws of *ahavat Yisrael,* or of the "love for the Jewish people," that Gershom Scholem found tragically lacking in Hannah Arendt (how much more so in Donald Trump!). And, on the other side, the enormous metaphysical importance, for the Founding Fathers and their successors, of a symbol that implied that America, new as it was, was still bound to its Jewish spiritual roots, just as Rome had remained a Hellenic power in Polybius's mind.

And, finally, when weighing policies, one cannot simply disregard the fate of real Jews living real lives, not only in Israel but in the United States as well. To celebrate imaginary Jews who, on the Judgment Day, will arise from their graves to serve as escorts for Christ's return is fine. But it would be so much better to honor, respect, or even protect the real flesh-and-blood Jews who are not just standing around waiting but are fighting for their dignity and, too often, for their very survival! From this point of view, Trumpism falls far short of the target. Before Trump, particularly on American campuses, there was a powerful anti-Semitism of the left centered on promoting a boycott of Israeli products to protest the country's presence on the West Bank.

Segments of the left (notably the extreme left) have taken advantage of disdain for, or hatred of, Israel to galvanize other "victims," making the anti-Semitic potion even more dangerous.

And the friends of Israel will not soon forget the U.S. abstention in the UN Security Council just before Christmas 2016, allowing an anti-Israeli resolution to pass: to them, this clearly conveyed that the outgoing administration had resolved to conclude its second term with an unprecedented slap at the Jewish state.

But does anyone need to be reminded of the rising tide, in nativist and white supremacist circles, of a right-wing anti-Semitism that purports, since Trump, to reopen debate on the real color of the skin of Seth's and Jacob's children?

Or of the flood of tweets and retweets during the presidential campaign, where every strain of lunacy seemed woven into a single story of hate and criminality?

Or of the bile brewing in the depths of so many souls, which, during the election, began to flow forth, bearing along a flotsam of jokes about gas chambers, calls to reopen "the ovens" for the Jews of New York and Los Angeles, and assorted conspiracy theories?

Does anyone need to be reminded how, each time the attention of the new president of the United States has been drawn to the return of the oldest form of hate in one of the few places in the world where it seemed to be rejected and contained, that president has chosen to avoid the issue?

An example. His press conference with Benjamin Netanyahu, held during the latter's visit to Washington in February 2017. An Israeli journalist asked the president about the worrisome uptick in anti-Semitic acts in the United States. Instead of responding, the president rambled, as we have come to expect from him, about his astounding success. And, returning finally to the question posed, he observed, with a blank look and in a mechanical tone, that many "bad things" indeed happen in his country but that he will be, you can count on it, a president who cares about "peace." That catch-all idea of the many bad things that happen in the country was not far from his disastrous declaration six months later, after the riots in Charlottesville, when he put on the same footing the racist violence of neo-Nazi sympathizers and the strong reaction of counterdemonstrators.

Another example. Another press conference a day after the first one. Another journalist, this one from an American Jewish weekly, asked Trump what the administration intended to do about the growing number of synagogues being attacked, Jewish schools evacuated, and community centers terrorized by bomb threats, thus far thwarted or faked. What was the president's reaction? "Sit down," he said, cutting off the reporter in mid-question. "I am the least anti-Semitic person you've ever seen." Then, when the journalist attempted to resume his question: "Quiet! Quiet! Quiet!" he commanded, leaving the audience dumbstruck. And the least-anti-Semitic-of-people-or-presidents could find not a single word to explain how the America of Martin Luther King and Elie Wiesel intended to check the wave of anti-Jewish hate that was spreading across the country at a rate not seen since the 1930s.

Not to mention the strange set of circumstances that resulted in the omission from the president's remarks on Holocaust Remembrance Day of any reference to the six million Jews exterminated by the Nazis. It was the first time since the observance was created that those words were dropped. With this fillip of ancillary offense: when the White House was asked about the sudden disappearance of Jewish names and about how those names had become a mere detail among the innumerable victims of Nazism, the functionaries whose job it was to serve up that day's "alternative facts" tried to shift responsibility for the mistake onto a speechwriter who was, they saw fit to observe, a "descendent [sic] of Holocaust survivors."

In a column in the *New York Times* published the day before Trump's inauguration, I quoted some table talk by the future president, reported in a book by John O'Donnell, a former chief operating officer of Trump's Atlantic City casino: "The only kind of people I want counting my money are short guys that wear yarmulkes every day."

I also quoted Trump's campaign remarks to a gathering of donors from the Republican Jewish Coalition: "I know why you're not going to support me! It's because I don't want your money."

And I recalled a 2013 tweet storm in which, desperate to show that he was "smarter" than the "overrated" comedian and commentator Jon Stewart, Trump saw fit to rip off the mask behind which stood Jonathan Leibowitz, the Jewish name Stewart was born with.

In the same column, I compared Trump to the emperor Diocletian, a former swineherd who had been mercilessly teased by the students of a yeshiva run by Rabbi Yehudah.

Later, after Diocletian had become emperor, he summoned the rabbi, who lived in the distant city of Banias. He arranged things so the rabbi would have to travel on the Sabbath, then tried to boil him in the post-travel bath customarily provided to permit guests to cleanse themselves after a dusty voyage. And when, at last, he received his visitor, he said to him with spite: "Just because your god performs miracles, you think you can scorn the emperor?"

This story seemed to me a good metaphor for America today, where, as in Rome, the triumph of nihilism can enable a swineherd—in other words, anybody, no matter how inarticulate—to become emperor.

But more than that, it is a good allegory of the double-edged favors, the scalding baths, and the poisoned apples, proffered by a humiliated man, eager for revenge, who decides to show Jon Stewart and his fellow Jews that he is indeed stronger than they are.

I am trying to be measured.

I know that blind, obsessive, and unsubstantiated criticism of President Trump, when coming from a European, can be a disguised form of the old anti-Americanism. So I weigh my words.

But I have not changed my opinion.

Where Trump is concerned, I believe we are witnessing the "anti-Semitism of resentment" that Freud and Sartre identified.

Jews appear to those who harbor this resentment,

including Trump, as representatives of an "elite" that patronized them for too long and against which they will take revenge once they are in a position to do so.

And so I am addressing the Jews of America and the world who might not see the trap here; I am addressing those blinded by Trump's inconsistent, unreliable, and ultimately dangerous benevolence; I am addressing everyone who seems to forget that, no matter how often the forty-fifth president of the United States expresses his love for Israel, reasserts his solidarity to its prime minister, and reminds us that his grandson is a Jew, he will always be a bad swineherd who reveres only power, money, and glitz and could not care less about the miracles, the calls to study and intelligence, that are the proper genius of Judaism. And to all those people, to those who, in a word, refuse to understand that entering into an alliance with *that*, bowing not to Pompey or Assuerus but to Diocletian, is to deny oneself, to betray one's vocation, and to risk becoming no more than a shadow of oneself, I wish to say that, at the very best, they have put themselves in the position of Joseph making an alliance with Pharaoh to protect his brothers. But we know how that story ends. Just as a new pharaoh "arises over Egypt" who "does not know Joseph" and reduces his descendants to slavery, so, sooner or later, a new president will arise over America. Which will lead, according to the Talmud, to two equally tragic scenarios.

The "new pharaoh" may be new only in a metaphorical sense. As the Talmud clearly puts it, he is the same pharaoh who has "turned bad"—a turncoat. In which case, the unpredictable, occasionally benevolent Trump becomes another Trump and turns against an Israel about which, at the core, he cares not a whit: Israel, in this case, has everything to fear from the president's legendary but cynical "pragmatism."

Or the newcomer may indeed be a newcomer, another pharaoh altogether who arrives to take the place of the present one—and he will associate the Jews with his predecessor, whose cause and destiny they so recklessly embraced. In the United States, as elsewhere, the strength of the Jews lies also in the scrupulous maintenance of bipartisan balance. Their great wisdom has always been to avoid too ostentatious an embrace of one party over another. And they are a perfect illustration of the famous law of Cardinal de Retz, according to which "one abandons ambiguity only at one's peril." I suggest that it is terribly dangerous for Jews to forget this very old and prescient lesson.

But, for the time being, the heart of the matter lies elsewhere. Donald Trump's exaggerated invocations of Jerusalem no longer have much to do with the case of real Jews who are being attacked by white supremacists—and even less with real Jewish culture, a culture that preaches the humanity of others, kindness to strangers, and a willingness to clothe the naked, feed the hungry, and offer water to the thirsty.

These concerns and principles were the culture of the Pilgrim founders. But they are the creed, too, of the Jews who have played such a large part in building modern America. And it is to be feared that, with the banalization, negation, or, at best, the metamorphosis of the living name of Jerusalem, the second engine powering the empire, the good empire, risks being shut down.

4

Jeremy Bentham and the Web

So be it, one might say.

But aren't you crying over yesterday's empire?

The tears you're shedding for Virgil, for Jerusalem, for Europe's parapets, aren't they coming a bit late, since the real empire is busy exerting its global domination through GAFA—Google, Amazon, Facebook, Apple—which were born on the West Coast of the United States and have become states within a state, empires within the empire? These gigantic firms, which have three-quarters of the planet in their grip, aren't they now the very face of the empire, insolent and unabashed? This America that you are not the first to say is in decline, isn't it the center of a revolution that has changed the face of humanity and made the United States more dominant than ever?

Yes and no.

Yes, because these companies—though they are so completely unrooted as to be almost hydroponic and are governed by no law, not even that of the United States—are, in their culture, language, and metaphysics, unmistakably American, as was Hollywood, that prodigious factory of planetary myths invented a century earlier by a handful of recent arrivals from Europe.

And yes, because with the Internet we are still in that same immaterial, gravity-free, borderless, nontemporal space that, after 1945, gave birth to the first American empire. No doubt that space has been rearranged. Perhaps its volatility and fluidity have edged even farther into the abstract, becoming still more weightless and ethereal. But, just as one had to cross only a few streets to get from Churchill's Cabinet War Rooms to a still-powerful financial City that would eventually extend to Wall Street, so today's America has had to take but a short step to translate the language of Churchill and Milton Friedman into digital form; to move from the Pentagon and Wall Street to Palo Alto and Seattle or from Arpanet to the Internet; and to route across the planet, using the wires and networks it had already built, the fantastic inventions of GAFA.

But at the same time, no.

I stand by my diagnosis.

First, because the most notable phenomenon of recent years is that one of the rising powers, China, wasted no time in curtailing access to the networks made in the U.S.A. and preferred to invent its own versions—not GAFA but BATX: Baidu, Alibaba, Tencent, and Xiaomi.

And especially because, from the perspective of the battle for democracy and law that I believe to be the noblest vocation of the United States; from the perspective of strength for good, or at least strength for the lesser evil that the country has managed to remain, however haltingly, through the two and a half centuries of its brief history; from the perspective of the Peshmerga that I so admire and from their perches overlooking Nineveh; from the perspective of the Syrian Kurds now being cornered and massacred by the Turks; and from the perspective of the wretched of the earth and, by extension, of all the peoples of the world, the new empire with a digital face alas changes nothing of the general movement of American retreat and decomposition. Indeed, it even promises further renunciations that, in some ways, will be even more calamitous.

AT BOTTOM, WHAT IS THIS ALL ABOUT?

What really happened in the short time that it took for a band of young people, working in their garages and dorm rooms, to dream up and put into practice the equations and protocols that underpin this electronic empire of

GAFA, a system of influence and control whose strength is gradually coming to be seen as greater than that of the old empire and its heavy equipment? And what are the concrete implications of those events for the peoples of the world and, already, for the people of the United States?

The story began like a fairy tale offered up to the rest of the planet: the giddy opening of infinite spaces and labyrinths of intelligence; the vertiginous feeling of having all the known world (and perhaps Hegelian absolute knowledge) within one's grasp; the joy, for those living at the edges in remote villages or peripheral nations, of gaining access to globalized methods of socialization and personal growth.

It was an incalculable contribution to the prosperity of the most deprived nations on the planet.

For people who previously had no collective importance, who were forbidden to speak or even to possess a narrative and a story of their own, who never had the right to the flicker of existence that consists of writing their name in an archive of solid matter, for those whom Michel Foucault called "infamous" in the sense that they are deprived of fame or reputation, for all of them the fairy tale promised a new possibility of expression and the freedom, for the first time, to record that expression, as well as the revolts, hopes, and dreams that accompany it, into the new register of the Net.

Thus was born, as everyone knows, the Arab Spring.

Thus, many other insurrections against assorted dictators.

And so it was—as every humanitarian activist knows—with the movements of solidarity that now come together on the Internet in the blink of an eye: solidarity with the starving people of the Sahel, with the Rohingya in Burma, and with a young Iranian woman condemned to death by stoning; or the miracle of men and women living in the farthest reaches of sub-Saharan Africa who learn to count, read, and communicate from apps on their smartphones.

But then things began to go wrong.

And the machine, revving up, began to produce effects, first in the West and then in the rest of the world, that were embedded in the program but did not function as expected.

One example is the trap of social networks, which in fact de-socialize, offering the illusion of supposed friends who friend us with a click and unfriend us with another, their accumulation ultimately signifying that we no longer have any friends at all.

There is the fake treasure and authentic fool's gold that is measured not in bitcoins amassed on the Dark Web, but in "likes" and "followers," who supposedly raise the value of our existence.

There is the summoning in our minds, at will and with no need to leave the couch, of places that we can visit, like a Xavier de Maistre without the imagination, from within the four corners of a smartphone. Taking this as raw material, we have the invention of a neocosmopolitanism stocked with images, not of the oddities with which we came face-to-face on our escapades, but of ourselves endlessly reflected in the mirror of those oddities. Yesterday's travelers would collect fetishes, curios, bits of a frieze purloined from a Khmer temple, fascinating stones. In this new world, which seems made to lead not to a beautiful book but to a gallery of Instagram selfies, we collect ourselves, getting high on narcissism repeated ad infinitum, and we reign over a world nearly stripped of its substance.

And then there is the jettisoning of memory that the Internet's memory makes possible. It fell to one of my old French professors, Michel Serres, to identify this new pathology, which he dubbed "the syndrome of St. Denis," an allusion to the third-century martyred bishop climbing the eponymous hill north of Paris carrying his decapitated head under his arm. In this case, it is not exactly our head but our memory that we have been holding in the palm of our hand or carrying in our pocket since unloading onto machines the task of restoring to consciousness the information, encounters, and scraps of memory that they can indeed summon a million times faster than we can. And so we forget.

I, too, have Facebook, Twitter, and Instagram accounts that I try to use to advance causes that are important to me.

I, too, use Google every single day of my life, and I know the extent to which its search engines, its nearly infinite libraries, and its tools have altered—for the better!—my work as a writer.

But I am keenly aware of the perverse effects of these tools.

IT IS ALSO IMPORTANT TO RECALL THE ROLE THAT THE DIGITIzation of the world has played in the global offensive against the will to seek and find truth.

For this, people blame Trump. Or Putin. Or Erdogan.

They see the origin of the invasion of "fake news" in the cynicism of a handful of populist leaders who, in the West and elsewhere, have claimed the Orwellian power to decide where the truth lies and where it does not, leaders who understand how useful the systematic manipulation of history and its narratives can be in their power struggles at home as well as in their foreign adventures.

Digging a little deeper, one enters the philosophical realm and blames, haphazardly, "deconstructionism"; the historicization in modern times of the desire for truth; or, in an all-encompassing stroke, Nietzschean perspectivism and its postmodern and structuralist successors.

Those arguments have some merit, no doubt.

But the charge against the postmodern philosophers and, before them, Nietzsche, seems misguided. By what does one measure the value of a man, asked Nietzsche, the "fool of Sils-Maria"? By his capacity to free himself from the grip of idols and delusions. By the quantity of thought that his "great health" is able, or unable, to "bear" and to "seek." By his quality as a "holy sage" capable, as Nietzsche said in *Untimely Meditations*, of staring down the most negative and painful of what life can deliver—capable, that is, of living with the truth. That truth may be out of one's grasp. It may be unbearable. One may die or become mad in the course of one's quest for it. But not to appreciate Nietzsche's "horrible worker" trying, alone, without God, to be accountable for the brief glimmers of a truth that he tracks with the energy of Rimbaud pursuing the "dawn of summer" and, in the end, embracing it, is to have understood nothing of the adventure of this genius.

And as for the others, as for the great names of the deconstructionist moment, as for the philosophers who were my masters at that last temple of knowledge that was the École Normale Supérieure of the late 1960s in Paris and who taught an entire generation what we call thinking— what a profound misunderstanding! To take hold, that misunderstanding depends on a desire for revenge on the part of mediocre thinkers and manufacturers of clichés. It requires a willful misinterpretation by lazy minds breezing through the strange shopping mall that the intellectual world has become. It implies a world that can find nothing better to do than to tar and feather the great names of the last century, to paste their faces on wanted posters (more like unwanted), or at best to hold a clearance sale:

"Everything must go!" But the reality is that the ultimate aim of the deconstructionists was never anything other than to search for the truth. To cite just a few examples: Jacques Lacan's *Prosopopée de la vérité*; Jacques Derrida's "we need the truth, it's the law" from 1972; the maddening quest for scientific precision and processes that runs throughout Louis Althusser's entire corpus; and the final lectures given by the dying Michel Foucault, lectures devoted precisely to "parrhesia" and the courage to seek and speak truth.

But, above all, I am convinced that to get to the heart of the disaster and understand the origin of the anti-truth offensive, we have to invert the order of the reasons (the exception does make the rule!) and look *first* at the technology side; and we must focus not on a form of metaphysics or politics that happens to be equipped with a technological means of implementation, but rather on a new and mighty technology that is pulling a politics and metaphysics in its train.

The chain of causality is as plain as can be.

Take the nearly infinite number of voices that the triumphant Internet makes it possible to put out there.

Combine it with the invasion of the Web by a torrent of dammed-up speech that has waited too long for this moment to permit wasting even the tiniest bit of the new rights and the joy that goes with them.

The Web then becomes a throng, a free-for-all, a headlong pursuit of the self, where everyone shows up with an opinion, a conviction, a complaint, and a "personal truth."

And, at the far end of a process rendered inaudible by the roaring tinnitus induced by the tweets, retweets, posts, and shares with which the Web bombards us, we see that all and sundry—innocent or villain, good or bad shepherd, lord, killer, easy prey, or punching bag—begin to demand for their newly asserted truth the same respect that formerly was accorded to the brave old truth.

The point of departure was the equal right of all to express their beliefs; but, somehow, we wound up asserting that all of those expressions of belief are of equal value.

We began by saying, "Listen to me, and hear what I have to say." Then: "Respect my personal speech, whatever you may think of it." And we arrived at this: "Don't let me hear you say that your speech is better than mine or any other; don't try to tell me that, in this globalized chatroom where we're all competing to have our say, there might be a ladder of truth."

We believed we were democratizing courage and truth, qualities so dear to Foucault late in life.

We thought we were giving to all friends of the truth the technical means to make their contribution to the adventures of consciousness and knowledge with as much audacity or restraint as they wished.

But that is not at all how things worked out! What we called forth was a banquet. On the table lay the naked body of truth. Driven by a cannibalistic impulse, we set to pulling it apart. Each of us stitched together a patchwork of beliefs and certitudes from bloody shreds that soon began to rot and stink. The banquet has become a farce, a motley bazaar where it is forbidden, under penalty of being hauled before the international court of anti-discriminatory struggle, to defame the Harlequin's coat of one's neighbor. And in it we saw the return, minus the Hellenic elegance, of the perversity of the Sophists who so violently opposed the nascent philosophy of Greece's golden age.

Like the ancient Sophists, the sophists of the digital age assert that what for so long had been known as "the truth" is really a shifting shadow, since the puppeteers, like the rest of us watching the show, possess no more than random bits of spoiled meat.

In that night where all illusions are gray, in the dark and clamorous profusion that the Web and thus the world has become, man alone, we shout, echoing Protagoras, is the measure of all things, and the truth of one man is as good as that of his neighbor.

So the bullheaded populist braying his fake news at the Republican convention in Cleveland and the Harvard genius whose homeland is the world turn out to be more closely related than we thought. Trump and Zuckerberg, though they probably agree on nothing, are the two blades of a pair of scissors that is cutting the fabric of truth to ribbons.

BUT THERE IS EVEN WORSE.

And, here, we are approaching the vital and, alas, mortal principle of the new empire and the reasons why, by definition, it holds no promise for the Kurds of Erbil and Kirkuk, for the Syrian victims that the Trump administration was in such a hurry to abandon to their fate and to Assad, or for any of the other peoples who have suffered, and still suffer, persecution for seeking to share the best of the empire's values.

The Greek Sophists, remember, claimed to be model democrats.

In reality, they were the allies and quartermasters of the tyrants.

That was the lesson of Philostratus, the Greek rhetorician of the second century BCE who served in the courts of the Roman emperors Septimius Severus and Caracalla. Philostratus showed us in *Lives of the Sophists* how Herodes Atticus, seemingly a philanthropic builder of stadiums, aqueducts, and theaters, in fact had the soul of a despot.

But it had already been Plato's lesson in *Phaedo*, where the philosopher ranks nine types of men by their relationship to the wisdom that is, precisely, what distinguishes man from beast: the sophist ranks second to last, just above the tyrant, whose precursor the sophist thus appears to be.

And it is the whole story of the trial in which the most noble of the Athenian philosophers became the expiatory victim of tyrants, of the six thousand Heliaia convened in plenary session to hear the case, *but also* of the reigning sophist thinking.

So, if there is one last reproach, and perhaps the principal one, that may rightly be leveled against the creators of the Internet, those distant descendants of Protagoras and his ilk, it is that they paradoxically moved in step with the tyrants, provided them with weapons and fuel, and offered up for the taking an unprecedented and insidiously effective tool.

First came the smartphones that one human in three now carries in his or her pocket and that provides so many little pleasures that it seems nearly impossible to imagine living without them.

Then came the "identities," the "profiles," the "accounts" on Facebook and Twitter, which, in combination with the smartphone, are like so many tiny, embedded informers capable of recording, storing, and transmitting the data that users leave there.

And it turns out that the data that subjects willingly supply, the profiles that they update so assiduously, the diary that is compiled based on the sites we visit, the photos we like, the comments we leave in forums that are supposedly managed in a cool way, from continent to continent, by the benign masters of the Web—it turns out that all that material is indeed centralized, processed, sorted, and put in the cloud in the form of databases, where it is used in two ways.

Commerce first. GAFA seem to have found the holy

grail. For the first time in the history of humankind and its alchemical dreams, they have acquired the fabulous power to transform into gold, literally, the dust and dirt of trillions of tiny acts, humble confessions, and mute expectations. And, for the hip young Americans who reign over this universe and deploy unlimited energy to keep us hooked up to their machines, using all the tricks of the most sophisticated behavioral psychology (2,617 caresses—tap, type, swipe, click—per person per day, according to a study by the application Dscout), for these libertarians of silicium and, tomorrow, graphene who, once I have chosen to pay to read Dante or to listen to David Bowie, offer to relieve me of the burden of having to choose ever again (decide once; the algorithm will decide forever), what a windfall, what a mother lode, what a boon!

But right behind commerce creeps power, posing a much more harrowing question. Because for all those who, down the centuries, have pursued the ideal form not of government but of police power, GAFA's systems offer a windfall of equal proportions. Take our comings and goings, our associations, our good and bad thoughts, our possibly seditious intentions, our *liaisons dangéreuses*, our deviances. Consider all those little piles of secrets that dribble in, each morning, to the interior ministries of all of the world's democracies, and, of course, to the autocracies as well. So much for the grunt work formerly done by two-legged agents! Good-bye to old-fashioned spycraft with its risks, breaches, and heavy hands! All of that is now built right into chips that are both minuscule and immense. At least in principle, and if the GAFA of today were not ruled by scrupulous women and men, it is all available to the NSA, the CIA, the FSB, and the Guoanbu. And the most extraordinary thing is this: none of it occurred behind our back or without our cooperation. It was with full awareness, with an innocence and enthusiasm that no theoretician of voluntary servitude could possibly have imagined—not Étienne de La Boétie, not Wilhelm Reich— that we turned ourselves into suppliers of data. When any of us surfs the Web, when we do a search or make a purchase, or even when a Turkish, Egyptian, or Russian dissident communicates via Skype or FaceTime, we leave behind us fingerprints that Big Brother will use in any way that pleases him, whether it is to cash in or clamp down.

It is said that one of those kids, namely Mark Zucker-berg, gave some thought to becoming the youngest president of the United States before concluding that the power he would thus acquire, the power to relaunch the great Virgilian and metaphysical adventure of his country, the power to determine whether nations make war or peace in Kirkuk, Syria, and elsewhere, seemed to him hopelessly old-school when compared with the power he already possessed: the power to amass wealth equal to that of half of the states of the world; to throw himself into the race to explore planets; to influence, manipulate, and, at the end of the day, to "make" a democratic election; to get into the heads of several billion people and, once there, to think, desire, and decide for them—and to monitor them as they had never been monitored before.

A PERSONAL RECOLLECTION.

In the early 2000s, I became friends with Jean-Baptiste Descroix-Vernier, one of the French kings of the fast-emerging Internet.

It was he who persuaded me that a committed writer really had no choice but to establish a presence on social networks. We cooperated to mount a campaign against the stoning, in Iran, of Sakineh Mohammadi Ashtiani. Another against the appointment of an anti-Semitic Egyptian ex-minister of culture to the post of director-general of UNESCO. Yet another on behalf of the first protesters of the Tunisian Spring. And for that I will never be able to offer sufficient thanks either to him or to the astonishing machine that the Internet also can be.

He was one of those people whom we had begun calling geeks.

With a computer as his only companion, he lived on a houseboat in Amsterdam. On it he worked, played, read, Skyped, and sometimes slept. In short, he spent most of his time there.

A character right out of Robert Musil's *The Man Without Qualities*, he lost himself in his weights, measures, and algorithms, without ever losing sight of the fact that, in another life, he was the last of a line of peasants from the

Dombes, near Dijon, in the center of France, a legacy that led him to spend part of the money he earned buying up land that his forebears had worked as humble share-croppers.

As an added distinction, he was, at least at the time, the only French CEO to be ordained to the priesthood in a very private ceremony attended by the cream of the French stock exchange, a French president, and hirsute, tattooed bikers sporting portraits of Elvis on the back of their jackets. He was becoming a Gallican priest, and because Gallicans in France are a tiny group with no fixed place to worship, it was necessary to hire a Protestant church for the ceremony. The end result was that the lot of us, believers and nonbelievers, mighty and humble, stood together for hours, in the cold, waiting for our friend, who was laid out on a stone slab with his hippie locks over his shoulders and a tonsure at the top of his head, to finish reciting the litany of the saints, which we had thought was reserved for warding off or mourning major calamities.

Jean-Baptiste was the head of a company whose employees—whom he called "ninjas"—he recruited in courtrooms around the world, where the first great hackers were being prosecuted. As soon as a new case was publicized, as soon as he heard about an Internet genius who had cracked the codes of a multinational or of the central bank of Ukraine or Belarus, or as soon as his network of informers presented him with the case of a hood who had succeeded in breaking into an intelligence agency, this agoraphobe would hop on a plane, park himself in the courtroom, observe the accused from a discreet distance, form a judgment about whether he was Scarface or Lupin, Dillinger or Robin Hood, decide if he was lost for good or ready for redemption (applying the knowledge of souls that he had learned in the confessional), and, when the latter was the case, introduce himself to the judge, offer an employment contract, and redeem the Fantômas of the Net.

One day I asked him what, exactly, his little army of penitents was working on.

And this is what he told me.

He was like a Mormon, but in reverse. It was not dead souls that he and his ninjas were looking for, but living desires. On news sites, online sales sites, chat rooms, and anywhere else that living, desiring beings left traces of their needs, appetites, whims, and vices, he was harvesting data that he intended to turn immediately into money.

After a long silence, he showed me a tiny USB stick. "It's all here. Millions of human beings revealed by their desires, classified according to their origins, their beliefs, their inclinations, fixed or fluid. And you know what? When I go, I have only one wish. I have no kids, not many friends, but I do have this one last wish, and that is that this stick should be destroyed. Because I know how much harm it could do if it fell into the wrong hands. I know what a diabolical tool it would be for a new Hitler, Stalin, or ordinary dictator, this collection of humans sorted like animals, graded like peas, and laid out like things."

Chamath Palihapitiya, a former vice president of Facebook, would say years later that the programs he helped create "are ripping apart the social fabric" and that he would not allow his children "to use that shit."

Bill Gates, too, admitted that he would not allow his children to use smartphones until they reached the age of fourteen.

A short time before his death, Steve Jobs told his biographer, Walter Isaacson, that his own children had never touched an iPad.

The coolest schools in Silicon Valley are unconnected, low-tech places where the teachers have gone back to using blackboards and chalk.

Barack Obama told a conference in Paris on December 2, 2017, that Mark Zuckerberg, again, felt "real concern about the role" of the golem that he had unleashed.

Google CEO Sundar Pichai said to Lauren Goode, on a Recode podcast, that one of the first things he does "every single morning" is to read a "physical paper."

Ruth Porat, chief financial officer of the company and, in her personal life, a devoted philanthropist, generous fund-raiser for humanitarian causes, and trustee of prominent academic institutions, told me in a recent encounter that nothing was more precious to her than a great work of literature.

And consider *Tablet*, an online intellectual hub run by Alana Newhouse and a clutch of young intellectuals who tout the need to disconnect from the zoo of net: for them, too, the future is in paper.

But my French friend had said it all.

He had described perfectly the submission of speaking beings to the all-encompassing technology devised by a handful of American firms that is the new horizon, the new frontier of what America, through those firms, is offering the world.

He had illustrated the mutation of politics into biopolitics—that is, into the apprehension of man in his entirety, from the normal to the pathological, both clothed and naked.

He had put his finger on the triple effect—hedonic, economic, and possibly tyrannical—that Foucault had anticipated in his theory of biopowers but did not live long enough to see put into practice. (The "encroachment of death," in Nietzschean terms, prevented Foucault from becoming old enough to savor his bitter victory.)

Most important, by breaking the taboo, by pointing out the hypocrisy looming over the potentially tyrannical future of these friendly, entertaining, and seemingly harmless applications, and by speculating out loud that the two logics—commerce and control—could coexist or even be purposely linked, he had simultaneously described, named, and denounced the deception behind the smiling face of this latest avatar of the empire.

But now I come to the heart of the matter.

And here it is necessary to bring up the name of someone who is neither a French geek nor a GAFA head but rather an eighteenth-century English philosopher: Jeremy Bentham.

Who was Jeremy Bentham?

Though Bentham was a major figure in the history of Anglo-American thought, it was Michel Foucault who, in *Discipline and Punish*, brought him to the attention of many non-English-speaking readers, highlighting one of the philosopher's late-in-life projects.

Bentham invented a model prison that he dubbed the "panopticon," the chief feature of which was a central watchtower that allowed the guards to observe the prisoners detained in chambers radiating like spokes from the tower hub, without the prisoners being able to observe the observers.

Bentham conceived the simple idea that it is enough for a person to believe that he is being observed (and possibly seen through), even if the panopticon is empty, to get that person, without force and even without words, to bend and submit.

By extension, and because the principle applies not only to prisons but to hospitals, factories, schools, and any other location where humanity is assembled and ready to be domesticated, he is also the designer of a modern disciplinary system that is nearly invisible, requires no foremen or trustees, and therefore is that much more effective.

But for those who know Jeremy Bentham only through the panopticon, his larger contributions to philosophy are less appreciated. He was, first and foremost, one of those thinkers known during the English Enlightenment as a utilitarian. That is, as the expression poorly conveys, one who views the right to happiness as the first among the rights of man. And also one who bases the social contract not on fear, necessity, voluntary limits, or even the presence in the cornerstone of politics of a measure of metaphysical truth, but on happiness, happiness alone, the greatest amount of happiness that is consistent, for each person, with the greatest happiness of the greatest number.

Because of this principle, because, in nature as in the politics derived from it, nothing counts except the quantities of suffering prevented and of happiness delivered, Bentham was also a fierce proponent of individual liberty and rights; he was a strong advocate of the rights of homosexuals, which was rare in his day; he was, incidentally, the author of *Principles of International Law*, which presented a plan for "universal and perpetual" peace that is even more delectable than Kant's; and he was the proponent of a utopian world court that foreshadowed the present-day International Court of Justice and International Criminal Court.

And, finally, he was that "friend of humanity" who, on

August 26, 1792, for all the foregoing reasons as well as for two reform proposals that he had the honor of submitting to the embryonic National Assembly in Paris, was nominated by the Girondist leader Brissot (who devoted a chapter of his memoirs to Bentham) to receive the title of honorary citizen of the French Republic, just as it was preparing to proclaim the right to happiness: the same honor was bestowed on Thomas Paine, Anacharsis Cloots, Cornelius de Pauw, George Washington, and Alexander Hamilton.

Discipline and happiness.

Drunk on control and fastidious about welfare.

An eye that never shuts, that watches over bodies and peers into souls, invading their privacy—but all without compunction, in the name of universal felicity and with the assent of the subjects who are getting what they asked for.

It is the combination of the two that makes the system strong.

And it is this combination that will assure the system a future both radiant and terrifying.

Which is right where we are today!

If one sought to date the first appearance of the ambition to see all and know all that is at the heart of the American digital revolution, but which functions only, I repeat, in a climate of euphoria and apparent anarchy; if one were to trace to its starting point the genealogy of the machines that probe so deeply, though gently, into our hearts and minds that they seem a subtle tyrant, a domesticated god; if one had to name a single progenitor of the idea of biopower amiably taking hold of the *bios*, of naked life, of the raw intimacy of souls, of the body and spirit of each one of us, then the name that would suggest itself, the only one that marries the two seemingly contradictory imperatives of authority and sweet seduction, the only one to assert that human rights and surveillance, respect for freedom and the recording of our secrets, need not be in opposition, the only one that the congenial entrepreneurs of GAFA could have had in mind, even if they had never heard his name, is the firm-handed voluptuary that was Jeremy Bentham.

The old-fashioned empire had its theoreticians—among them Keynes, Adam Smith, Hayek, Schumpeter, and, more recently, Samuel Huntington.

The new empire that, on the whole, could not care less about stopping the Iraqis and Iranians in Kirkuk as long as it can keep its eye on them (and on their victims) bears the stamp of Jeremy Bentham.

5

Thus Spake the Empire of
the Eye and of Nothingness

But that's not the end of it.

And the truth is that its journey through the centuries, its encounter with the new technology and the extraordinary opportunities that it offered, transformed and refined the Benthamite mechanism in a way that could only accelerate the rise of the new imperial system.

For if there was one thing that neither Jeremy Bentham nor even Michel Foucault could have imagined, it is that the panopticon can be turned around at any time.

Operated from the top down, it gives GAFA, governments, and other actual or would-be major players full power to observe, monitor, and control those under their dominion.

But the paradox is that those at the top wield tools that are no better than those available to the people on the bottom, who, provided they are a little geeky or at least use the right websites, can be just as powerful as the people at the top.

To put it another way, the eyes of the panopticon are like bifocal lenses that superimpose two opposing views.

They are like the vocal tones that the ancient monks, who perfected reading out loud, found could either fall or rise—that is, could either be swallowed or projected up to heaven.

And, instead of passively allowing themselves to be watched, the lowly eyes take the initiative; they start watching, too, turning the imperative to see all back on those who conceived and promoted it; they turn their leaders into objects of insatiable and unforgiving curiosity; with the result that the watchers come to be watched, the informers informed on, the inspectors inspected, and the biters bitten.

In stage one biopolitics, the little people must submit to the law of the panopticon. In stage two, which features programmable smart tools, the machine also sucks in the bosses, the powerful, the dominators.

First it was just the convicts of, for example, the Philadelphia model prison. Then, gradually, the circle widened to take in the potential delinquents that we all are in the eyes of the Eye. Now it is the turn of elected officials, the elites, and those who think themselves above the law to be hauled into the yard to be scrutinized, exposed, and toppled.

Old-fashioned biopolitics—in other words, that part of modern biopolitics that functioned according to the old rules—wanted its subjects naked; in new-style biopolitics, it is the king about whom we want to know everything so that we can point and say, as in Hans Christian Andersen's tale, "He's naked."

This reversal has its good side.

The laying bare of kings, the possibility of seeing them, as in the tale, with their pants down, this new right delivered to the disenfranchised, to nobodies, to those who were called the sansculottes in the French Revolution for their lack of proper breeches, this power to expose princes, officials, prestigious people, and, of course, tyrants is central to the democratic idea and to democratic resistance.

And far be it from me to underestimate how much democracy in its most vibrant state, which is measured in rights newly acquired and freedoms dearly paid for, owes to the digital denuding of a Tunisian despot, a Ukrainian potentate, or all the major and minor creeps who think they have the right to exploit women's bodies in Hollywood or the subway: Was it not, after all, a machine of just that type that the ninjas of my geek friend from Amsterdam so generously ginned up for me in an attempt to apply these weapons of mass proliferation to my own causes and commitments?

But still.

The machine cannot distinguish between potentates and ordinary politicians. Or between good and bad causes. So, should we not worry about the parity in the energy it can bring to bear to topple a tyrant or to smear a democrat? Should we not be called to account for the delight we derive from both, which the neo-Benthamites calculate by the number of "likes" that accompany, like a fanfare, the arrival of each new scandal? And should we not be alarmed about the terrible damage thus done to the art of politics, now displayed solely in its worst manifestations? Hillary Clinton was politically killed when FBI director James Comey revived the matter of her emails ten days before the election. French president Emmanuel Macron was subjected to a grotesque and destructive manhunt in July 2018 after the press revealed that a member of his security detail, Alexandre Benalla, had been mixed up, without authorization, in a crowd-control operation during a violent demonstration on May 1.

Furthermore, how can we not be concerned when suspicion, accusation, and, ultimately, raids and roundups go out of control and are extended, for example, to artists? Before, you had to be at least a valet, as Hegel said, to steal a hero's boots. You had to be Norbert Elias to dare to reduce Mozart to his sociological status as a bourgeois artist adrift in courtly society. Today, we are all valets, and the sociological reduction of geniuses is conducted via Twitter.

And, again, the politicians. Are we so sure that the risk

of being observed always has the effect of discouraging, let alone blocking, abuses of power?

Remember that in good Benthamite theory, control and happiness go hand in hand. The nudity imposed on the powerful may serve less as an incentive to appear virtuous (I know they can see me naked, so I'm going to restrain myself) than as an inducement to let oneself go (how wonderful to be seen naked; why hold back?). Isn't that right, Mr. Trump?

Remember, too, that, in Andersen's tale, the emperor realizes that the two cloth makers have conned him by weaving an imaginary cloth; that the child and the rest of the people perceive him as naked not because they are stupid or malevolent but because he truly is naked; and that this in no way discourages the emperor from going ahead with his plans and imperturbably displaying his nakedness.

And finally, to take a current example, I note a more than paradoxical aspect of the campaign of digitalized neo-feminism launched in the United States before spreading to the rest of the world.

That campaign began by denouncing sexual offenses, calling out the perpetrators, and breaking the code of silence: and it is great.

The movement pilloried those who have lived for too long in impunity: and this is a deliverance; more than that, it is a true revolution, reversing centuries, if not millennia, of humiliations and abuses perpetrated against women.

But there is a deplorable aspect of the modern fable that, alas, is all too real; during all this time, the most notorious sexual delinquent in the United States, the man who bragged about grabbing women "by the pussy," whose own attorneys have acknowledged that he tried to buy the silence of women who had leveled accusations against him, remains imperturbably ensconced, like the emperor in Andersen's tale, in the fortress of the White House.

BUT THERE IS MORE.

In this globalization of the panopticon there lurks a second reversal whose consequences, as far as the metamorphosis of the empire is concerned, are going to be nothing short of catastrophic.

It is not only kings and their subjects who carry the little spy satellite around in their pocket.

You, I, and nearly everyone else—billions of human beings living on every continent and connected by GAFA or their Asian equivalents—have the personal and portable panopticon at our disposal.

The panopticon's eye, the eye that sees and goes farther, surveys all, the immense eye that tirelessly turns and turns, rolls and veers, not only can be reversed; it can also be diffracted, becoming like a fly's eye that is not content to examine things from top to bottom, or from bottom to top, but wants to see in every direction.

It was not long in coming.

During the span of time we were thinking about this third possibility, the neo-panopticon was made.

Everybody is gazing at everybody.

The voyeuristic impulse, far from stopping at scrutinizing groups of anonymous, undefined, and invisible people, and later at exposing the sins of the rich and powerful, has taken off at breakneck speed and is poking into the intimate business of anyone and everyone.

And this newly expanded Benthamism, spread horizontally and laterally, is creating a society of generalized indiscretion in which everyone spies on everyone else, where we join a social network to signal to our peers that they have the right to know everything about us and vice versa.

The parts are interdependent, of course.

And everyone gets something out of the game.

Because the princes had an interest in the big data of which each of us contributed a small part, they allowed us to rummage around in their past and present, their bank accounts, their private emails, their jobs obtained through family connections, their reading habits, and their love affairs.

Because their little piles of secrets fascinated us, we allowed the masters of the universe to transform our purchases, our travels (tracked to within an inch), and our sex habits into data that could be converted into wealth.

And, now, because, since the dawn of time, there has never been anything more exciting than rifling through the dirty laundry not only of the king but of our neighbor, we give permission to do the same with ours.

There is in this a circular voyeurism that is at the very least obscene.

It is a corrupt bargain in which the parties agree to share the right to spy on each other and, ipso facto, to denounce each other.

And this alliance of the naked, this symbolic exchange of the pleasures of seeing and being seen, is the title deed of a new type of social contract in which it is no longer our freedom or our will that we are agreeing to limit, but our privacy.

Oh, what a lot of time we wasted with Rousseau, the masters of the social networks and their addicts seem to be saying.

And what a lot of time we wasted trying to reform and redeem people and to encourage them to aspire to greatness.

We should have listened to Bentham the prophet, the Heidegger of the new technology.

We should have let people be what they were—namely, beings guided by pleasure and constant affirmation of self.

We should have remembered that, as pleasures go, there are few more widely shared than the desire to peek into one's neighbor's undergarments, and that being allowed to gratify this desire surely merits a small sacrifice of sovereignty.

The system behind this mutual nondiscretion pact is not entirely democratic, since this dictatorship of transparency, the hold that it gives each over the others, is much closer to what the Greeks called demagogy.

Nor is it an oligarchy, since the masters of the universe are, now, the first to be exposed to this underwear-diving mania, this prayer answered.

It is not a monarchy or the degenerate form of monarchy, which, for the Greeks, was tyranny: for that, there would have to be a clandestine conductor, a central plotter, in the watchtower of the new panopticon.

No.

It really is a new system.

This system invented by a handful of companies, under which most of humanity now lives; this system in which one may trade, at any time, the right to see all for the obligation to show all and in which the bond holds only under the condition of general participation, is a heretofore unidentified form of government; it cannot be found in the classifications of Polybius or others; I am tempted to call it *scopocracy* in recognition of the dominance, in it, of the scopic impulse.

BUT, AGAIN, TWO QUESTIONS PRESENT THEMSELVES.

First, does the bond hold?

Is it possible to bind together a society, *a world*, on

the idea that people are only what they are and never will be otherwise? That they have, by definition and as a consequence, nothing to hide? That any enterprise aimed at making them transparent and getting them to cough up their secrets is legitimate?

Scoffers will point out that this temptation runs afoul of one of the oldest laws of history, one laid down at least as early as the tragedies performed in Epidaurus and Taormina: do not look too hard into the mirror that is the animal body of your peers lest ye be blinded.

Those of us who are even more jaded will bring up Saint Augustine's views on "lust of the eyes."

Or the story of the people of Sodom, whose fatal crime was to have demanded to see, just to see, the angels staying in Lot's house.

Or that of Moses, who, Rashi tells us, has but one moment of doubt, just one. It is the day after he killed the Egyptian in great secrecy. But two Hebrews are there and know that Moses killed him. They threaten to reveal the deed. And because he has been unmasked, because he has been seen killing, and because there are two informers, just two, among the people of Israel, the thought crosses his mind that the entire people is no longer worthy of being saved and that the promise made to the patriarchs is null and void.

Without going back that far, there was a French filmmaker named Henri-Georges Clouzot who, in a masterpiece entitled *Le Corbeau* ("The Crow"), demonstrated the ravages that the unchecked voyeuristic impulse can wreak in a society.

I met Henri-Georges Clouzot a few times.

It was with Yves Montand and Simone Signoret at the Colombe d'Or in Saint-Paul de Vence, where Clouzot spent winter and spring in a little apartment tucked away at the end of a walk lined with broken columns in a corner of the grounds of the auberge.

He wore the perpetually frightened look of a man who has committed the mistake of plumbing the true underside, the underworld, of contemporary history and has never recovered from the shock of what he saw.

One night, under the fig trees, because I wanted to get to the bottom of the trial inflicted on him after the Liberation of France, he told me this: a film, a mere film, portraying a town in occupied France that surrendered itself to the obscene pleasure of informing on each other; the death, crime, madness, and obliteration of social ties that ensued like a match put to a line of powder; for having shown that, for having uncovered that dirt, for having dared to uncoil the implacable Bickford fuse that, from its start with an anonymous letter scrawled in a scullery, ended up dynamiting an entire city, the filmmaker is insulted, accused of being an accomplice in the crime he decries, deemed an affront to the myth of forty million resisters, burned in the public square, dishonored.

His script was set during the Occupation in a tiny city of France.

But, changing the scenery a bit, the tale could also be told in one of those glass-walled houses erected by the GAFA masters from aluminum and teak in the hills of California or alongside the waters of Washington State, where men are no longer expected to be wolves but rather crows.

And its lesson applies, indeed, at any remote outpost of the empire of the eyes that is spreading across the planet; it applies anywhere where this new Benthamite social contract has taken on the force of law, with its injunction to say all, see all, and show all; with its new certitude that what is real is not what is rational, as Hegel believed, but what is visible and exhibited; with its way of believing to be true, like a postmodern, obscene Doubting Thomas, only human wounds, gaping and bleeding, into which we are invited to insert our fingers and eyes.

First question, then.

What if the Web, with its links, graphs, and branching trees, has become a man-eating plant?

What if the panopticon is a cluster bomb?

We talk constantly about the viruses that might disrupt the Net, infest it with bugs, bring it down. But what if the Net itself were the virus? What if it is the Net that is gnawing away at the links that bind people? And what if the bug threatens those old faces that seem to be fading away, like sand figures on the shore of the Net: the individual subject and the idea of a fraternal society?

———

WHICH BRINGS ME TO THE SECOND QUESTION.

The one, essentially, that I posed at the outset, where I was worrying that an America that has so conspicuously turned its back on the appeal of Virgil and Jerusalem was in the process of saying good-bye to the good and beautiful side of its imperial calling.

I was expressing the fear that America could become just another country, bigger than most, more powerful, grappling with myths that were a little more outsized than the others, but all in all a country like another, with a president who, seventy-five years ago and in the grip of the original America First, might not have waged war against Nazism.

And I was wondering whether it was even possible to continue to describe as an empire a country that has given birth to a mechanism of power as decoupled from political prescription and regulation as the GAFA machinery.

Well, the response is here.

It is complicated and perhaps even contradictory, but here it is in two propositions.

The first.

Yes, we are still dealing with an empire.

About a country whose pipes carry such a large share of the world's speech, one that dictates the rules of conduct of three-fourths of socialized humanity, furnishing them with a ready-made contract that, until it implodes, apparently provides enjoyment and stability, about a country whose child-kings in California are inventing the universal language of which humanity has dreamt since the dawn of the history of empires—about that empire one can say, more truly than ever (transforming into an observation the boast that Britain formerly applied to itself), "America rules the waves."

And perhaps the country has never been as strong, as paradoxically imperial, as it has been since displaying, in Kurdistan and elsewhere, so many unmistakable signs of saying good-bye to all that. One thinks of *The Invisible Man*, the 1897 novel by H. G. Wells that appealed so to America's imagination. It is when a being has made himself invisible, Wells said, that he is at the height of his power. Never has he had such license to steal, deceive, or kill his peers than once he has disappeared. And nothing is better than screams coming out of nowhere to disarm your fellows, to sow mortal terror in their hearts, and to bend them to your will. So goes today's empire. It cannot be ruled out that it has never been so dominant as it has been since it gave to everyone on the planet—without any shouting from the rooftops, without even showing itself—the mandate and the means to make each other speak, sing, and reveal themselves, since deciding that it would be content to propagate its waves, good and bad, over the seas, the soil, and the summits of all the world.

We thought it had evaporated, but it was just vaporizing itself.

We imagined that it had cut its tethers to the ground, but it had mutated into an aerosol whose particles (that is, its usages and techniques) are penetrating the most remote corners of the planet.

As an example—the last, the most terrible example, and for that very reason the most eloquent—I cite the relish shown by the radical Islamists since the torture and execution of Daniel Pearl, for filming, editing, and (until the world finally rose up in protest) YouTubing their decapitations. The Nazis erased the evidence of their acts. The Stalinists, without ever attaining a refinement in denial equal to that of the Nazis, did not brag about their gulag. And as for the Cambodian perpetrators of the third great genocide of the twentieth century, they, too, operated behind closed doors, with executions carried out in secret and followed by summary burials in pits. Why, then, did the Islamic extremists operate in the open? What accounts for the fact that their crimes seem to them complete only once the entire planet can witness them? And is that exhibitionism not all the more curious given that it runs counter to twin traditions in the long history of the very Islam that they so loudly proclaim—a distrust for images and an apparent preference for modesty and reserve that, in this instance, could not have been more squarely violated? It may be objected that these are bad Muslims ignorant of the major role of iconoclasm in Islam. And it would not be hard to find scholars (or "students") of religion who would explain sagely that if they are permitted, on the one hand, to veil their women, and, on the other, to indulge in the unmitigated pornography of exhibiting the bodies and faces of their victims, it is because they do not see any common ground between the impurity of the former and the inhumanity of the latter. I do not doubt that there are Islamist sophists who would argue that specimens of inhumanity such as Jews, "Crusaders," or Arab homosexuals (including those filmed waiting to be pitched from the rooftops of Mosul) deserve whatever they get; but it is impossible not to also see in this exhibitionism a measure of mimicry of the West, whose influence on the Islamic radicals is, on this score, obvious from the fierceness with which they deny it. Film everything. Show everything. Set up ultra-high-tech studios in the center of Mosul to produce montages that aim for Hollywood quality and will be freely downloadable from the Periscopes, Facebooks, and YouTubes that deliver the omnipotent Western visibility. My hypothesis is that there is, here, a dark fascination with the telling all, the seeing all, and the showing all that are the new laws of the empire—and that ISIS, in a way, carried into the Muslim world our own thirst for transparency.

But here comes the second proposition.

What is the formula for the new-generation empire?

How can we best describe an empire that limits itself to spreading its vapors, plumes, and waves over the world's surface?

And what are we to make of an imperial form that is so indifferent to its content that, for so long and without too many qualms or scruples, it consented to carry over its waves the filth that ISIS produced?

One could say, of course, that history repeats itself and that nothing much has changed since Hegel and Melville: America was fluid; fluid it is becoming again. Submerged it was, then, in an ocean of land; submerged it remains in the evanescent immensity of the Web. Even its tears, when it remembers to cry, are crocodile's tears—invisible, imperceptible, like filaments or fog.

But one is also reminded of Edom, which is, in the Jewish tradition, the name applied to the last empire. Edom is "drunk on Nothingness," says the Maharal of Prague, but reigns over the nations with a strictness that is all the more implacable. In other words, it is simultaneously all and nothing. It is all because it is nothing. It is nothing, because it is all. It has nothing special to say because nothing opposes it any longer and it extends over all the ancient kingdoms. It no longer has to be this, that, or anything else, because it no longer has any particular message and has become another name for the world.

And one is reminded, once again, of Nietzsche. One thinks of what he, too, might have labeled the empire of nothing. It is not nothing to want nothing, he said. It requires a force dark and negative, but a force all the same, perhaps the strongest of all forces, to reason right through to the end about nihilism and the absence of meaning. It takes a really firm hand, he might have added, the most powerful of superpowers, to seek to establish, as have the masters of the Net, a kingdom that has no frontiers or territories, no palaces or castles, no temples, no judges, no culprits and no innocents, no good, no bad, not even a real king (none of the GAFA chiefs has ever wanted to be king, as they never tire of telling us), and no good ideas or faulty beliefs (are not all thoughts of equal value once they can dance on the waves?). But it is an untargeted force. A hand with nothing to grasp. It is a very powerful empire, but it rules over specters and is a force for nothing, for no message and no values, that exerts itself over "the last men." And, even when it raises its voice, gets worked up, and roars, it now roars into the void, having nothing to propose, impose, or defend.

That is where America is.

Vigorous and silent.

Preeminent but mum.

It is as if it had worked so hard to set the parts of its desire trap that it forgot how to make it speak and do the job it was made to do.

It is as if, in becoming not the world's policeman but the Web's, it had forgotten the most perilous but also the most precious and rarest quality it possessed: its will, from time to time, to speak what is just, free, and true.

And it is all happening as if the energy expended to stretch, as Arthur Rimbaud would say, from bell tower to bell tower, or from star to star, the ropes of the global panopticon had left it bereft of the time, inclination, or inspiration to support the cause of the people of the world.

Occasionally it emits a sound, but these are vague signals such as those that came out of the brief, abominable (literally, a thing apt to offend a god) episode from the battle of Kirkuk to the abandonment of Kurdistan.

We still see tweets floating like listless waves on the surface of the new Aral Sea that covers, these days, the formerly shining city on the banks of the Potomac; but, in the bristling of their hashtags, it is difficult not to see the hatchet wounds of denunciation and the stalag in which abandoned peoples will tomorrow find themselves confined.

The sky darkens over the empire and becomes, to borrow a phrase from Charles Baudelaire, "like an immense altar." The sun that lit a century of American predication becomes like a "long shroud" (Baudelaire, again) rustling no longer from the east but now from the west. The West still reigns but is no longer willing to say to the afflicted peoples of the world: "Sons and daughters of Troy and Jerusalem, of Aeneas and the Pilgrim fathers, we have climbed this hill, we have built and inhabited this city— and, today, in fear and trembling, uncertain of ourselves but with faith in our calling, we extend our hand to you."

And as it falls mute, other powers are awakening, raising their heads, and, in the chilly silence, beginning to speak.

PART TWO

FIVE KINGDOMS ON THE OFFENSIVE

6

The Earth Shook in Kurdistan

I RETURN TO KURDISTAN.

"Return" is not the right word, since I never really left it.

For the years of the Bosnian War not a day went by that I was not together in thought with the friends whose cause I had embraced. Wherever I was, I stayed abreast of the tiniest advance, the sometimes alarming reversals, and, too often, the deaths of comrades felled by snipers' bullets.

During the war in Libya, and then during the freeze, the convulsions, and the confusion that followed, when the very idea of an Arab democratic revolution seemed lost, I continued to make myself available—for an attempted mediation in Paris, for a summit in Tunis of actors of goodwill, for a secret meeting in Malta with a warlord who supposedly controlled the coastline from which boats loaded with migrants departed for the El Dorado of Europe, for a delicate negotiation with an Islamist militia that had just kidnapped my friend Ali Zeidan, the former prime minister, in the middle of Tripoli.

Similarly, not a day has gone by since my first report from Kurdistan in March 2014 without my thoughts returning to Sirwan Barzani, a general as brave as Napoleon's General Jourdan and whose soldiers, for two years, held the front most openly and dangerously exposed to the Islamic State; to the mustard gas victims whose wounds were so appalling that my camera crews and I could not bring ourselves to film them; or to the survivors from the bunker in the Zartak Mountains where the young, white-haired general Maghdid Harki, a man fond of quoting French revolutionaries Georges Danton and Camille Desmoulins, took a bullet to the head.

No. When I say that I am returning to Kurdistan, I mean that I wish to go back to those days of late September and early October 2017, when the destiny of the Kurdish nation and, through the butterfly effect, that of the world, hung in the balance.

And I would like to finish describing what exactly took place there, over several days, in the great vacuum left by the evaporation of the empire, at the borders of that pre-Columbian world without America that I felt we were entering.

I RETURN TO THAT BEAUTIFUL SUNDAY IN ERBIL WHEN PRESI-
dent Massoud Barzani, normally so reserved and reluctant
to show his feelings, confided to me, "It's done; I can die,"
echoing France's president on the day World War I ended
in 1918 and also Johann Sebastian Bach in the aria for alto
in the St. John Passion.

I return to that Monday when the Kurdish people celebrated in the streets of every town in the country: the
flames visible in the clear, dark sky were, for the first time,
not rockets, tracers, or shells trained on enemy positions
but fireworks and bonfires of joy.

I picture another Barzani, Netchirvan, the prime minister, who had never favored holding the referendum, as
he very nearly confessed to me once on the telephone. I
picture him some time before the scene I described earlier, in which he learned that the Iraqis' threats of a blockade had been put into action. This is the evening of the
day of the referendum, and we are in his office. He, too, is
happy. The handsome, clean-shaven face of a privileged
young man educated in international schools is illumi-
nated by a victorious smile that previously I have glimpsed
only in very old photos of him wearing a Peshmerga uni-
form. His look has become martial. And all of his strength,
usually held in reserve, seems fully deployed. No more
Mr. Nice Guy. So long to the obedient Western student
waiting patiently for independence to be granted. The

father of the nation, he tells me, has won. He willingly acknowledges that Massoud Barzani and the other old warriors were right in arguing that the Kurds had survived all their trials, crossed the Acheron a hundred times as victors or vanquished, and that, when a people is in that situation, when the worst is behind them, they have nothing to lose—and become invincible.

But I think back, too, alas, to that Tuesday, that Wednesday, to the days that followed, to each hour and every minute leading up to my departure. My mind returns to the reversal and to the sudden, generalized, disappointment. A clap of thunder. Another. Then more. Night was falling over Erbil. It happened so quickly, a lightning stroke. And the Kurds were branded once more.

THE FIRST TO SPEAK OUT WAS THE TURKISH PRESIDENT. ONE of Recep Tayyip Erdogan's European interlocutors had more or less convinced him that this referendum was not such a big deal; that Massoud Barzani was a reasonable man to whom he was bound by long and solid relations; that the worst thing for Turkey would be for Barzani to make an alliance with Turkey's Kurds and their political arm, the Partiya Karkerên Kurdistanê (PKK); but that was precisely what Barzani had wisely promised not to do.

The Turkish president had grumbled. Speaking from experience, he acknowledged that when hundreds of thousands have cheered you in huge rallies in Sulaymaniyah,

Dohuk, and Erbil, when you have raised such high hopes and are carried along by the people's fervor and yearning, it is difficult to reverse direction. But then, the following night, he saw on television scenes of the jubilant Kurds. And he glimpsed a few Israeli flags bobbing in the flood of Kurdish flags. In a fury, he called his European contact in the dead of night on the hotline reserved for emergencies and crises: "Treachery! Betrayal! Your harmless little referendum turns out to be a Zionist plot! I see only too well now who has been pulling the strings in this provocation, this farce!"

The following morning the Turkish press was full of the conspiracy, supposedly hatched in Tel Aviv. And, on the social networks of Erdogan's Justice and Development Party (AKP), and of Islamist groups affiliated with it, there circulated a photo taken on the day of the results, following the lunch that Massoud Barzani had organized for the international observers of the voting. It showed Barzani cutting into a big green apple, the symbol of sin, under the knowing and abetting eyes of the former French foreign minister Bernard Kouchner, to his right, and, to his left, myself. That photo was offered as inculpatory evidence, proof of the plot!

I tried to tell myself that this inveterate paranoid had done something similar in August 2013, when he declared at a rally in Rize, his hometown in Anatolia, that he had irrefutable evidence that Israel and the "Zionist agent" Bernard-Henri Lévy were behind the military coup in

Egypt and the deposing of his "brother," President Mohamed Morsi. Questioned about the proof he claimed to have, he proffered a video of a public debate between the Israeli justice minister Tzipi Livni and me, held at an Israeli university during the war in Libya. The video showed a student asking me what should be done if the Muslim Brotherhood were to pull its chestnuts out of the fire of my activism and take power in Tripoli or Cairo. I responded in a learned, knowing tone: "That won't happen, but if it does, it will be necessary to block them using any and all means available, absolutely all."

That is the sort of "proof" Erdogan believes in to this day.

And none of that should surprise those who, in the summer of 2018, watched him declare that the failure of the Turkish economy, the collapse of its currency, the corruption of its administration, the incompetence of its civil servants—all were to be attributed to another such conspiracy, or perhaps to the same one.

NEXT TO BE HEARD FROM WAS THE IRANIAN PRESIDENT, HASsan Rouhani, who, we were told, had spoken with Erdogan by telephone the night before and shared his view that the Kurds' "adventurism" was leading to chaos. Ali Akbar Velayati, a former Iranian minister of foreign affairs who was now the diplomatic adviser to the Supreme Leader, Ali Khamenei, then described Barzani as a "fixer" (that was his word) for the criminal Zionists whose goal, following the dismemberment of Syria and Libya, was to dismember Iraq. The media in Tehran, in unison, upped the ante by calling for the Kurdish troublemakers to be brought immediately to heel.

Next up were Iran's two henchmen, Syria and Iraq. The former called repeatedly for a freeze on the results of a referendum that, as seen from Damascus, was creating "chaos" (I must be dreaming!) on the banks of the Tigris. The latter, ostensibly a federal state accountable for maintaining peace and security on the territory of its component parts, issued incendiary statements followed up by maneuvers of intimidation that observers quickly understood as portending a full-fledged military offensive.

Then Erdogan was back. Seeing that no one seemed bothered by his threats and that Washington was impassive, he took the opportunity to throw into the pot a few strong, blunt anti-American statements; a few others about Kurdish terrorism, which he vowed to eradicate with the same energy he had applied to the Islamic State (!); and a cryptic reference to the "new Lawrences" who had supposedly misled Barzani into "casting himself into the furnace."

And then President Rouhani, discovering that anything could now be said, or even done, without rousing the U.S. administration, jumped in to announce that Iran, like North Korea, had just successfully tested a new midrange missile, Khorramshahr, capable of reaching Tel Aviv or Haifa. He let it be known that when war came with the Jewish state (only a matter of time), the Lebanese Hezbollah, thanks to deliveries from Tehran, would be able to send a thousand rockets a day raining onto Israeli territory. He also bragged about a substantial Iranian investment in an oil refinery in Syria.

Have we ever seen so many provocations in such a short time and without the West seeming to take the slightest notice? The United States would eventually react, of course. But too late. Much too late. By pulling out of the nuclear agreement with Iran. And by flexing its muscles in the face of a Turkish state that was breaking, one by one, its ties with its former allies. But for the moment, that's where things stood. The "Kirkuk moment" indeed.

THESE WERE THE KURDS' ENEMIES, YOU MIGHT OBJECT.

But didn't they have any friends (aside from the United States)?

Yes, of course.

Well, allies anyway.

And I am here to affirm that, despite claims to the contrary, the government in Erbil had the foresight to keep its allies informed about the timetable for the referendum and, to the extent possible, to obtain assurances of their support in case something went wrong.

But that is not how things worked out.

What surfaced was one of those unexpected occurrences, stealthy as an epidemic, which, when they present themselves, win over the most skilled virtuosos of politics and history, as Machiavelli wrote.

Saudi Arabia was one of those possible allies. The Kurds, being the enemies of Shiite Iran—the enemy of the Sunni Saudis' major enemy—were their de facto friends. But it so happened that those September days were also the days when Mohammed bin Salman, the young and ambitious crown prince of the House of Saud, launched his first purge. No one could have imagined that this operation, limited to a handful of theologians and passing nearly unnoticed at the time, would lead the prince six weeks later to eliminate, in the space of one night, like Nero, eleven of his fellow princes, four serving ministers, and more than thirty high officials of what immediately became the ancien régime. But he himself knew it, of course. He was aware of being engaged in a terrifying struggle that left him no room for error or distraction. And I know that when President Barzani, just a few hours after telling me that he was now satisfied enough that he could permit himself to die, telephoned the crown prince to remind him of their agreements, of the long-running relationship between their families, and of Riyadh's interest in preventing the Shiites of Tehran from realizing their historic dream of a crescent of faith and force stretching from Lebanon to Bahrain and passing through Kirkuk, Mosul, and Damascus, Mohammed bin Salman was fighting on another front and had other lions to tame. In fact, he

was dealing with housebroken cubs who allowed themselves to be rounded up without a fight and caged in suites
in the Riyadh Ritz-Carlton. But on the accelerated schedule that governs all coups and that now governed him,
during those days that were counted in hours when one is
aware that victory belongs to those whose hand is steadiest
and who focus on one thing at a time, the crown prince
was simply not there for the Kurds.

Russia was not an ally, nor was it an enemy. It had too
many interests in Kurdistan for the Kremlin to disapprove
of the Kurdish desire to remove itself from the shaky sovereignty of Iraq. At the height of the crisis I learned that,
several months before and amid great secrecy, Kurdistan
had responded to its looming economic strangulation by
ceding to the Rosneft oil company, known to be close to
Vladimir Putin, the formal ownership of the old pipeline
that led west to the Turkish port of Ceyhan and that was
its sole link to the outside world. The night I learned of that
sale, I endeavored to fight back my anti-Putinism. I disre-
garded the fact that I was on the list of French citizens pro-
hibited from visiting Moscow. I inwardly asked my friends
from Kiev to forgive me for the sacrilege I was about to
utter. And I explained to one of the Kurdish president's
advisers that inevitably there come moments in the history
of a people when it is permissible to make a deal with the
devil and that, if they had a way into the Kremlin, now was
the time to exploit it.

Contact was duly made with Putin on the evening of

September 27. He had planned to be in Ankara for dinner with his "friend," Erdogan. Everyone in Erbil expected that he would use the occasion to urge moderation and calm, for these were in Russia's interest. After a long wait, the media announced that the two acolytes would issue a joint statement. The people of Erbil waited in anticipation under a giant screen set up in a café in the old city, in the shadow of the citadel. I was there as well, hanging on every word from a handful of friends, who themselves hung on the words of the TV announcer. But, to our huge disappointment, we learned that the two presidents spoke not about Iraqi Kurdistan and the impending war, but of their intention to implement the Astana accords on Syria. In other words, Putin did indeed raise the subject of the Kurds. But not these Kurds. Not the ones in Kirkuk who, in a few hours' time, were going to be cut to pieces by the heavily armed Iranian-backed militia. He had raised the matter of the Syrian Kurds who, of course, were also facing the threat of an ethnic cleansing and massacre. And it is possible that, for those Kurds, he provided a small reprieve from the Turkish irregulars who, in and around Afrin, were on the move and waiting for their moment. But the war in Syria was "his" war. And it was this other Kurdish war that would determine Putin's success or lack thereof in the Great Game that had begun again in the Near East. There had never been any question that he, any more than Mohammed bin Salman, would disperse his forces and take the side of the besieged people of Kirkuk.

Putin had his own agenda. Erdogan had his. Both within the context of their Syrian priorities. And, as thick as thieves, they wasted no time divvying up the field once the fake Hercules in the White House had withdrawn.

Lastly, there was China, which was neither friend nor foe. But, as I learned soon after in New York on the occasion of the screening of my documentary, *Peshmerga*, before the United Nations General Assembly, China had, at the time of the crisis in Kirkuk, been the most aggressive player blocking France's attempts to have the UN reiterate its recognition of the historic rights of the Kurdish people in both Iraq and Syria. China's underlying motives were different. The duel with the United States was raging. In the struggle of the titans for planetary supremacy, the climax seemed near and, in Beijing, a turning point appeared imminent. And in the dead and the dying of Kurdistan the Chinese saw three things.

When we are poised to become the world's leading economic power, they reasoned, we are not going to burden ourselves with the fate of a small, superfluous people whose victory or defeat will in no way change the order of things. Second, we note with great interest that this accursed people is the most faithful ally in the region of the nation that formerly was the richest on the planet and that this nation is not coming to its rescue. Third, we see in this the sign of a political and moral weakness that it would be a shame not to exploit by rushing into the breach that the retreating empire has just opened up. And that is why, in each of the great theaters where its rivalry with the United States was playing out, China used those days in September, and the days and weeks that followed, to rack up more points than it had scored in a long time. With new boldness, it reaffirmed its One Belt, One Road project. It reassured European leaders that they should not see in the project a twenty-first-century version of the Marshall Plan. It joined the very select club of powers possessing expertise in cyberattacks and the manipulation of democratic elections, interfering in Australia and New Zealand as the Russians had already done in France and the United States. It even treated itself to the luxury of trying to play referee, or perhaps white knight, in the wrestling match between Donald Trump and North Korea's leader, Kim Jong-un. And, on October 18, at the Communist Party congress, it announced that a "new era" had dawned and that the country was now looking toward "Horizon 2050."

ONE SHOULD ALWAYS BE WARY OF THE LENSES THROUGH WHICH one views the world.

And there is indeed a heightened risk, when looking at history through the prism of a specific situation, of developing the Perpignan railway station syndrome (it was "always at the Perpignan railway station," Salvador Dalí joked, that the "most brilliant ideas came to me"), as well as symptoms of a mild form of paranoia (since I am in

Perpignan, I declare Perpignan to be the center of the world).

But at least the prism can lead one to see things that one otherwise would not have seen.

At least it casts a light that reveals aspects of the world that, without it, would remain in shadow.

And, in the murky shadow of these events, in their scramble and crush, and in their seeming contingency, what the eye of the Kurds saw, and what it allowed others who had access to it to see, was this.

Not, of course, a global plot against a people who were being betrayed once more.

Not the romantic image of all the forces of evil arrayed against martyred innocence, as in an ancient tragedy.

Not even the bad luck and bad timing of a people who had not foreseen that their referendum would overlap Catalonia's or that it would come just at the time Mohammed bin Salman was preparing his purges, Vladimir Putin was pressing his advantage in Syria, and China was ushering in a new phase of its One Belt, One Road initiative.

What we saw was a distracted, preoccupied America and five actors taking advantage of that distraction: one to hasten a purge; another to advance a pawn on the chessboard of a world undergoing Sinification; a third to eliminate a group of military officers who most definitely were not going to be forgiven for plotting a coup the year before in Istanbul and Ankara; a fourth to increase its violations of the cease-fire in Donbass (in three years of war, never had there been so many as in those weeks of October); and a fifth to take additional liberties with the nuclear agreement it had signed with the world.

An America that went quiet and five pretenders who, in Kurdistan itself (Iran, Turkey) or elsewhere in the world (China, Russia, Saudi Arabia) spoke out and concluded that they could do as they pleased.

A West that was offering yet another demonstration that it was willing to abandon its own values, following on similar demonstrations of abdication in Crimea, Syria, and in the defense of human rights—and five kings who had begun dreaming of a decisive revival after a heavy but fitful sleep that had lasted decades (Russia), a century (Turkey), or several centuries (Iran, the Sunni Arab world, China).

Of course, there were countries that were in no way reflected in the mirror of Kurdistan—some large (Egypt, India, Brazil); some small but endowed with an outsized role (such as the United Arab Emirates, the anti-Qatar, that is one of the first lines of resistance against Salafism and jihadism in general).

There were other wars, some terrible, on which the Kurdish event had no influence, including the war in Afghanistan, where the Taliban was again taking the upper hand.

Moreover, the five kingdoms are not of the same importance and it would be absurd, for example, to put depleted Iran and immense China in the same category.

In some cases, the kingdoms can make alliances of convenience, such as Erdogan and Putin papering over their differences in Syria; or Erdogan, on the eve of a visit to Paris, supporting the mullahs in Iran by insisting that popular demonstrations against the regime in Mashhad, Doroud, and Najafabad were Iran's "internal affair" and that it was regrettable that "people from outside" had come to add "provocation" to "sedition."

They can forge new links or strengthen existing ones— such as Putin and the Iranians affirming and reaffirming their "strategic" resolution to fight "American unilateralism" together and to lighten the sanctions on Tehran; or Xi Jinping promising, after the U.S. pullout from the Iranian nuclear accord, to come to the rescue of an increasingly isolated Iran.

Unexpected and surprising events may occur, such as the first-ever visit to Moscow of a Saudi head of state on October 4–5, 2017, at the very moment of the Iraqi-Iranian attack on Kirkuk. That visit, conducted with great pomp, resulted in the signatures of fourteen commercial protocols, including one for the supply of S-400 missiles.

Still others may occur that promise to weigh heavily on the state of tomorrow's world. Putin had already received China's support after the occupation of Crimea. Moscow was already China's leading supplier of oil and gas, and China was the leading investor in Russia's faltering economy. But the year 2017 ended with a string of occasions on which the two powers congratulated themselves and each other on their growing partnership and the deep compatibility of their two pet projects, the Eurasian Economic Union and the One Belt, One Road Initiative. In April 2018 we are treated to the extraordinary family photo of Erdogan, Putin, and Rouhani posing shamelessly, despite their divergent interests and historic rivalries, on the eve of a summit on Syria. And, last but not least, in August 2018, as the value of the Turkish currency plummets, we see the same three (with the Chinese president and the emir of Qatar in the background) supporting each other and beginning to reflect on how, through their trade, they can escape the "dictatorship of the dollar."

In still other cases, enmity will endure—notably, that of Iran and Saudi Arabia, which will remain locked in a death struggle that is as old as Islam itself and that will be inflamed by quarrels surrounding Qatar and the war in Yemen.

And, finally, Saudi Arabia, the leading actor in the Sunni Arab world, is still (and until further notice must be considered) an ally of the United States, despite the October 2017 visit to Moscow, and despite its recurrent support for terrorism.

But all that is secondary.

The most important thing is that, when this story begins, all five actors are on the move again, sometimes separately, sometimes in unison.

The essential elements are the tectonic forces at work beneath a series of misunderstandings and calculations too numerous to be ascribed to chance (which the Greek historians knew was Necessity's other name) and that were shaping a new regional configuration.

What struck the witnesses to the Kurdish crisis so powerfully was an event that had been brewing since the United States began to forget that it was the culmination of a civilizing project born in Troy, Jerusalem, and Rome, where its constitutive values had been formed: that event demonstrated that history had not ended for everyone; it proved that tragedy was making a comeback, stealthy and noisy by turns, along five paths that it had not been expected to take; and it was easy to see that at the crossroads of those paths there had formed a sort of revisionist or revanchist front composed of five countries bent on redrawing, in their favor, the global map of authority and power.

7

Herodotus's Trap

THESE FIVE AWAKENING COUNTRIES, PLEASANTLY SURPRISED that history seems ready to repeat itself, these five kings, standing simultaneously on the balcony and in the street during this Kurdish version of the Battle of Jena, marvel as they see themselves mounting the horse of an emperor who seems to each of them to look just like him. These five kings have three traits in common.

THEY ARE, FIRST, THE HEIRS TO SOME OF THE OLDEST EMPIRES the world has known.

Not all of the enemies of the democracies are former empires.

North Korea, which seems to pose a fearsome threat not only to the West but to the world as a whole, has never been an empire.

Nor has Pakistan, which I visited often at the time of my investigation into the death of Daniel Pearl and which remains, to this day, the same nuclear-armed gangster state.

Nor has Venezuela, a state that is a calamity for Venezuelans and a friend of the most shunned regimes (Pakistan, of course, along with North Korea, Iran, Russia, and others just as odious), while also being the architect of the farcical "Bolivarian alliance."

And among the former empires, among all of the peoples who, hostile or not, have yielded at one time or another to the imperial impulse that Nietzsche (in *Twilight of the Idols*) said can be the crowning glory of politics when it aspires to be great and to avoid the shopkeeper's spirit, there are degrees of difference.

Some have been tiny: the Phoenician empire consisted of trading posts; Sweden's and Denmark's were limited to nearby conquests.

Others were vast but brief: at the beginning of the thirteenth century, Genghis Khan's empire of the steppes was larger than those of Alexander, Charlemagne, and Rome; but it was also more ephemeral, lasting barely a century before being swallowed by the Persians and the Turks that it had supposedly vanquished.

Others, such as the European colonial empires, were

too criminal to become the stuff of legend: objects of dispute, yes; of nostalgia for some and revulsion for many more; but nothing capable of sustaining a national religion.

These five, by contrast, the five that were active in and around the Kurdish theater, the five forces on the move—the Turks, Iranians, Russians, Chinese, and the Sunni caliphs—the five powers bent on revising the international order and preparing to show their hand (each at its own pace) in challenge to the United States and Europe, have the distinctive characteristic of being custodians of the most legendary examples of empire and of being, right up to the present, passionately inhabited by this imperial memory.

I remember attending a conference at the Second Foreign Languages Institute in Beijing in 1986, during my very first trip to China. I discovered that it was forbidden to mention the early dissidents and awkward to mention Mao and those who surrounded him in his later years. But the Cultural Revolution had not erased the memories of the Hans, Mings, and Qings, nor of any of the Sons of Heaven and empire builders into whose shoes President Xi Jinping would place his feet when, thirty years later, he invited his people to follow him in the "the great rejuvenation of the Chinese nation."

I remember a day in Libya in May 2011. I was on the Misrata front. The shelling from Mu'ammar Gadhafi's forces was so heavy that I had spent the morning at the bottom of a pit dug into a dune and converted into a bunker held up by pieces of scrap lumber. To kill time, my friend Suleiman Fortia, who had accompanied my team and me on the crossing from Malta, delivered a long, breathless monologue, jumping from one episode to the next of what to him was clearly a single story in which the ongoing battles in Libya were merely an echo. His voice barely dimmed toward the end of what had become, in his mouth, a song to defy the tumult outside. The story recounted how, in little more than a century and without any real military superiority, armed only with their faith, Muhammad and his successors had built an empire that stretched from Arabia to Mesopotamia and Persia; extended into Syria, Palestine, and Egypt; crossed Bukhara and Samarkand; vanquished the heirs to the Roman Empire in the Maghreb and Spain before moving fatally toward Tours; and defeated the Chinese at the Talas.

I remember another friend, with whom my friend Gilles Hertzog and I flew clandestine missions over Visoko during the Bosnian War. At the time, he was studying philosophy at Istanbul University. During the darkest hours of the conflict, he helped us transport (this time by road) telescopic sights for use by the defenders of the Bihac pocket, which was surrounded by the Serbs. He was a Francophile, an Anglophile, a Judeophile, a friend of humanity, and a proponent of Turkish recognition of the Armenian genocide. But if there was a subject on which he was unstoppable, one on which we liked to get him started at the outset of the critical phase of a mission, it was the history of the Ottoman Empire. On one occasion we were in the car we rented at the airport in Split, having driven through the night so as to arrive precisely at dawn at the isolated checkpoint on a rural road, where a bribed militia member let us through. We then had to look for the abandoned farm where we were to leave our precious cargo. This was the moment when anything could happen, including interception by a UN patrol. (Several months earlier, the UN had declared the area around the city a "security zone.") And as Gilles and I, hearts pounding, peered through the mist, which was not dissipating fast enough to allow us to make out the stream, the grove of trees, or the bombed-out house that were to be our signs that we were approaching the rendezvous point, our friend—possibly to bolster his courage; possibly because, as the Turkish adage goes, there is no surer way to make a mirage disappear than to summon up another one; or possibly just because we told him that the subject interested us—recounted for us the moments of glory of an empire that, five centuries before, in the time of Suleiman the Magnificent, had reigned over the homelands of Jesus Christ and of Socrates, over the former capital of the Eastern Roman Empire, and over the lands from which Alexander's march had departed. That empire had extended to the gates of Vienna, to Sarajevo, to the Indian Ocean.

I remember those who were called dissidents in Russia, some of whom, alas, have recycled themselves into mouthpieces of Putin's power. Many of them, beginning with Aleksandr Solzhenitsyn, were moved by the idea of the sacred mission of Holy Russia, which, at its apogee, reached the Baltics, Ukraine, and Belarus, encompassed Poland and the Grand Duchy of Finland, and ran out to Alaska and the far removes of Central Asia.

I have an Iranian friend, Amir Jahanshahi, who has not been back to Tehran ("officially," he says) for nearly forty years. From bases in London, Madrid, and Paris, he lives in a world of high finance in which nothing seems to exist except for the disembodied movements of the markets. This man, the descendant of an illustrious Persian family, was the principal backer of the domestic opposition to President Mahmoud Ahmadinejad after the contested election of 2009. Together we organized demonstrations in support of union leaders, filmmakers, writers, and others persecuted by the Iranian regime. But then I watched him change. He began to assert that the regime had "attained a maturity that allowed it to reform itself from within." He was grateful that Shiism had "prevented the Ottomans and the Arabs from dominating his country." He praised Iran for setting itself up as the "protector of all Shiites," thereby contributing to the "stabilization of the region." But he has one characteristic that survived this singular change of direction, and that is the joy that fills him whenever the conversation takes a turn that allows him to bring up the splendor, the greatness, and the past majesty of what, strangely, he never refers to as "Iran" but always "my country." It does not matter who is around. Any listener will do. A word, an allusion, a vague, polite question ("So

you're Iranian? Tell me about the situation in Iran . . .")—
these are all so many openings on which he seizes with the
eagerness of a lover. How many times have I heard him
extol (always with slight variations that make me think
that the story might be even more extraordinary the next
time around) the peak of excellence to which humanity
rose when the gods placed their fingers at the midpoint of
the colossal Persepolis Terrace, where the king of kings
received the emissaries of subject nations; to describe the
flank of Mount Behistun into which Darius had carved, in
three languages, the history of his conquests; to evoke the
mosques of Isfahan, where, André Malraux said, the blue
of the tiles matched that of the sky in order to suggest
paradise; to revisit the imperial bazaars of Shiraz and Ar-
dabil, whose splendor is equaled only by those of Athens
and Rome combined! When thus engaged, my friend's
handsome, wolflike face, which his long residence in the
West seems to have stripped of its Achaemenid mask,
displays an unrestrained smile, an especially bright gaze,
and an air of undefinable superiority that is more than
two thousand years old.

In all of them, the same pride.

In all of them, the same understandable self-respect.

For, in all of them, there is exactly the same sense of
being borne on the back of an incomparable past to which
they will always be loyal.

————

BUT HERE IS THE SECOND CHARACTERISTIC THAT THE FIVE KINGS and their subjects share.

They all have, even today, a clear, self-effacing, and thoroughly resigned awareness of the fact that the greatness of those empires, their incontestable munificence, the authority they exercised over the world, did not stop them from being destroyed and disappearing from the face of the earth, probably never to return.

Is that the lot of all empires?

No doubt.

For those who have studied the repeated enigma of triumph, decadence, and fall of the great collections of nations that we call empires, it is almost a natural law.

For Rousseau (*The Social Contract*), the empire succumbs when it has reached its maximum strength and the "social bond," stretched, begins to loosen.

For Montesquieu (*The Spirit of the Laws*), it is when the empire has expanded so far that it no longer has anything to fear from the outside world, when it is swimming in "too tranquil waters," that it disarms—and yields.

For Nietzsche (*The Genealogy of Morals*), it is when the empire, like Bismarck's Reich, feels that it need no longer fear any enemy and encounters no "contradiction" capable of testing and tempering its "necessity" that it loses its force and collapses.

For Gibbon (*The History of the Decline and Fall of the Roman Empire*), it is "prosperity" that, like a rank culture medium or a bad apothecary, "ripened the principles of decay" that it contained within it. In the case of Rome, those principles were the loss of the ancient gods and the evil genius of Christianity.

And then there is Oswald Spengler's *The Decline of the West*, published a century ago. Beyond its chief focus (the West and its inevitable downfall), the book offers a general model inspired by Nietzsche but also by Goethe and his passion for botany. Human bodies, Spengler said, are like plants. The bodies of societies and cultures are, even more than those of humans, composed of seeds, saps, branchings, and inevitable etiolations. In time, like humans and plants, societies and cultures also return to dust. And, yes, there is a human botany that dooms strong civilizations to wither, to degenerate into softer cultures, to sink into nothingness. The Austrian novelist Robert Musil did his best to debunk this mix of Baroque determinism, scientism in the mold of Molière's Dr. Diafoirus, and Byzantine organicism. But, from Arnold Toynbee to Paul Kennedy and Samuel Huntington, from Raymond Aron to Charles de Gaulle (who borrowed a little of Spengler's conception of the nation), and even Franz Rosenzweig, the brilliant author of *The Star of Redemption*, who believed *The Decline of the West* to be the most powerful piece of political philosophy since Hegel, it remains firmly fixed in modern minds.

In the present case, we are not dealing with the West but with the decline and fall of the five kingdoms.

It is to them—Ottomans, Chinese, Arabs, Russians,

and Persians—that the announcement has come, as in the Gospel of John: "The hour is coming, and is now here."

My Turkish, Libyan, Russian, Iranian, and Chinese friends—those that I have mentioned here and others that I have met on these five stages over half a century—have this in common: they have spent the bulk of their life with the twin certitude of being the heirs to an unequaled imperial past but also the inconsolable survivors of a catastrophe that they know to be irremediable.

China survived the sack of the Summer Palace, of course. But until very recently I had met very few Chinese willing to bet on the resurrection of the Garden of Perfect Brightness that was so dear to the emperors of the Qing dynasty. In my youth, the Hundred Flowers and the Great Leap Forward were the order of the day. Then came the Cultural Revolution, which was cultural in name only, since its goal was to cut ties with everything cultural and anything past. To our ears, the slogan "Let a hundred flowers bloom" echoed what Stéphane Mallarmé would have called "the ideal flower itself," the one that is "absent" from all earthly bouquets of bamboo, plum boughs, orchids, and chrysanthemums that Confucian scholars called the "four flowers of Junzi," which no one wanted to hear about anymore. Then came the campaign against the "Four Old Things," followed by the "Four Modernizations." The terminology could not be more eloquent. The goal was to lay the foundations for an unprecedented type of regime, one that combined the most savage capitalism with the most tyrannical aspects of socialism. In no case, however, was it designed to restore ties to the defunct dynasties of a forgotten empire.

When the Ottoman Empire was dismembered by the victors of World War I, the question was not whether, when, how, or by whose hand it might one day reappear. The only question on the minds of the witnesses to the event, and of all those who endeavored, for a century before the arrival of Erdogan, to build a modern Turkey, was when, exactly, the empire had begun to die. Was Vienna the bridge too far? Was it the emancipation of Greece and the philhellenic enthusiasm of European elites? Did the end begin even earlier?

The same fatalism can be found in Russia, where the mysterious collapse of the Soviet Empire in 1989 was followed by an unconditional political and ideological surrender that appeared to be without recourse or appeal. It seemed that Russia might already have withdrawn from history, despite its façade of expansionism. One theory was that the Soviet system had been nothing more than an illusion without a future, a long delusion, the red tree hiding the forest of a moribund reality. People calculated how long it would take Gorbachev's countrymen to become a Western country just like the others. But no one dreamt of reviving old forms, of breathing new life into the mausoleum of the czars or the marble statues of Stalinism, or of bringing the spirits of the great boyars, the Cossacks, or the engineers of socialist souls back to the Kremlin.

A similar defeatism has pervaded the Arab world, where the centuries of splendor lay in the far distant past: Umayyads, Abbasids, Fatimids; and then, little by little *fitna*, fratricidal splits; the Ottoman steamroller; the flight backward in time to the Salaf, those "pious predecessors" whose names come to constitute a barrier against all the ferments of modernity and the germ of the Salafist movement that, according to the late anti-Islamist writer and academic Abdelwahab Meddeb, is one of the chief causes of the "malady of Islam"; and then the Nakba, the "catastrophe," which seemed to be the last word, one that signified to all that the imperial adventure was over, that henceforth it would exist only in dreams of an impossible return to a lost purity—or in terrorist action.

As for the Persian Empire, it, too, was a thing of the past. It, too, slept buried under the sands of the archaeologists. No one imagined that it might take off once more in conquest of the world or even of the Ummah. And the ultra-kitschy commemoration in 1971 of the twenty-fifth centenary of Persepolis, an extravaganza of fake splendor put on by the last shah, was not going to change Iranians' minds. A riot of imported gardens, imported for a king's ransom from Europe (particularly Paris). Tens of thousands of birds that were supposed to revive the song of the *simurgh*, the winged mythical creatures held to be immortal in Zoroastrianism (like the gardens, the birds arrived by the container load before dying in the heat of the desert). There were parades of praetorians done up in embroidered tunics, skirts, turbans, and tiaras in the shape of the caps worn by ancient Achaemenid warriors. All of which added up, everyone agreed, to a pathetic spectacle. It was this sort of circus, this Persian theater, that the Islamic revolution, coming seven years later, promised to sweep away.

When I was a philosophy student, there was a story that fascinated me.

It was that of Epicharmus, a philosopher and writer of comedies at the beginning of the fifth century BCE. Most of his œuvre is lost, but what remains includes (in addition to some scattered quotations) a paradox that was as famous among the ancients as those of Zeno.

The man who knocks at my door, goes the paradox, is no longer the man I invited, so I am not obliged to let him in.

The man from whom I demand repayment of a debt is no longer the man who contracted the debt, so he may rightfully refuse to repay me.

The sacred galley of Delos is said to be the same vessel that carried Theseus to Crete, but every one of its parts has been replaced at some point over the centuries.

And a city whose builders all have been forced, by war, domestic strife, or tyranny, to flee to a distant colony, a city whose inhabitants have lost all contact, even through oral history, with its legendary beginnings, that city no longer draws from those beginnings either substance or spirit—it bears the same name, yes, but it is only a name, a sign, a cinder.

My Turkish friend, my Libyan friend, my Persian friend, and the others were, without knowing it, the successors of Epicharmus, melancholic but resigned. They sang so well of the glory of their empire only because they imagined it a homonym for what it had become.

That was thirty years ago, ten, sometimes less.

The glory that inspired them was no more than dust and dimly glimpsed ghosts, a museum.

Nothing was more remote in those lands than the idea of a resurrection of the will, the representation, and the world of empire.

BUT THEN CAME THE EVENT.

This is the last shared characteristic of the five kings—and the most remarkable.

These abolished empires, these "calm blocks here fallen from some far disaster," these agglomerations of nations resigned to their collapse—all begin to stir again, to set themselves in motion, and, given the share of the world newly exposed by the American withdrawal, to dream, to take a stab at predication, to recommence the assault on history.

You do not see the Tunisians talking about raising Carthage from the ruins.

Or the Macedonians of the former Yugoslavia laying claim to Alexander's heritage, apart from their dispute with the Greeks over ownership of their name.

Nor a tungsten-rich oligarch from Ulaanbaatar going into politics and singing the praises of Genghis Khan.

But with the five, that is what is happening.

The great crocodiles of the Bosporus, the Tigris, the Euphrates, the Yangtze, and the Volga are squaring off against Little Boy; in the wildest of their schemes, they see themselves taking him down in one bite.

And the sign of our times is the thawing of those frozen words that we heretofore believed destined for eternal repose but lately heard gnashing, groaning, rising from the depths, taking shape and giving new life to the spirits of the conquerors.

One of the crocodiles—Erdogan—has too much to do (putting down coups past and future and rebuilding his army) to be able, for the moment, to acquire the means to match his ambition. But the intention is there. He is asserting himself in Syria through military support for the Islamist groups of the Al-Nusra Front and, earlier in the conflict, for jihadists affiliated with ISIS. He is asserting himself in Azerbaijan through an overly enthusiastic solidarity with his Azeri "brothers" who are at war in Nagorno-Karabakh against an Armenia still seen as the refuge of a people the world can do without. He is asserting himself in Sudan, where—on the last day of 2017, at the invitation of criminal-against-humanity Omar al-Bashir, and speaking from Suakin Island (which was Ottoman for three centuries)—he reaffirmed his intention to become "the lion of the Muslim world." He is asserting himself in Chechnya (partly against his "Russian friend") and in Cyprus (definitely against Greece). He is asserting himself in Palestine against Israel, which, during the fourth quarter of the twentieth century, Turkey had almost forgiven for having been "grafted onto Muslim land" but can no longer be tolerated as a "canker" on the historic body of the Ottoman Empire. And when Bosnia-Herzegovina abstains from the vote on the UN resolution condemning the transfer of the U.S. embassy to Jerusalem, how do the new sultan and his coterie react? What sort of argument do they make to shame the Bosnians for their vote? They invoke the idyllic time when Bosnia and Palestine were *wilayahs* of the same Ottoman sultanate and call for the return of ancestral solidarity.

Like Erdogan, Putin lacks some of the means he needs to back his pretensions. But maybe he has been luckier. Or more clever in his maneuverings. Or perhaps it is his deep experience in the intelligence services and its codes that enables him to decipher signs of weakness in his enemies. Whatever the explanation, he is not far from having quietly reconstituted the frontiers of the Soviet empire whose implosion was, in his eyes, the most significant geopolitical catastrophe of the twentieth century. Through the annexation of Crimea, he realized the dream of avenging the wrong done to his idol, Nicholas I, when he lost the Battle of the Alma and the Siege of Sevastopol. And, through the unstinting support of Bashar al-Assad, he gained a permanent presence in the heart of the Mediterranean, which the Great Russians have always seen as the mother sea. Last but not least, he has seized on the Eurasian plan born in the 1920s in the midst of fierce anti-Westernism and has mandated its reorchestration by his court ideologues—notably Aleksandr Dugin. Eurasianism is two things. On the one hand, it is the pan-Slavist umbrella under which Russia has long dreamt of being a third Rome, the center of Christendom midway between Europe and Asia. On the other, it is the sewing machine required to stitch together the great coat of the Turanian, Uralic, and Altaic languages that the linguists of the Prague Circle—Jakobson, Trubetzkoy, Mathesius, and the other scholars generally regarded as having laid down the foundations of the "structuralist revolution" in Europe— studied for their timbres, accents, ties to Sanskrit, and infinite migrations. The work of the Prague Circle is underappreciated, which is unfortunate. Not only because its members were great thinkers. But also because it is in their scientific work that the Putinists see the justification for the belief that Russia is not Europe but has always been the bearer of a distinctive civilization that could be the heart of an empire extending "from Vladivostok to Gibraltar." Through one of the complex twists with which the history of political ideas is replete, it is they who indirectly inspired the great opposition between the "global Land" that the country of the czars should be (once it is restored to its vocation), against the shrinking "global Island" of the United States.

With my Iranian friend I discuss just about everything. But one subject has become taboo. And that is the constitution of the Shiite crescent for which the Kurds paid so dearly. The stranglehold on Syria and Lebanon through Hezbollah. The undisguised support for the jihadists of Hamas, even if they are Sunnis. The plan to annihilate Israel, which the Revolutionary Guards will continue to embrace as a holy cause no matter how far the Arab countries lower their tone. The strange statement made on January 7, 2018, by Ali Shamkhani, secretary of Iran's Supreme National Security Council, evoking the historic links between his country and Pakistan and calling for the reinforcement, in the face of American "threats," of "bilateral cooperation" with Pakistan, notably in the area of "intelligence." The intention, ever more openly expressed, to have their share, whatever the price, in administering the holy sites in Mecca. The territories in Central Asia and the Ganges delta now alleged, mezzo voce, to be related somehow to Iran. In short, the taboo subject is the great return of Iran as a major regional force, as a possible leader of the Muslim world, and one day, perhaps, as a world power.

Those of the Sunni Arab countries that sympathize with radicalism obviously do not intend to be outdone and do not hesitate to provide the means to counter the Iranian offensive. Consider the role of Qatar, before and after its rapprochement with Tehran, in the promotion of the Muslim Brotherhood and the invention of Al-Qaeda. Or that of Saudi Arabia, at least until 2016, in financing and ideologically arming Wahhabism and terrorist organizations. (Of *that* there is plenty of evidence—from the contents of American diplomatic cables revealed by WikiLeaks to the confessions of the jihadist leader Zacarias Moussaoui, who declared in a sworn document from October 2014 that "Al Qaeda received donations from members of the Saudi royal family" and that "without the Saudis' money, we'd have nothing.") And, in Yemen, the recourse to a form of gunboat diplomacy that does not shrink from massacres of civilians or blockades of humanitarian aid to prevent the Houthi rebels from opening the way to the neo-Persians.

As for the Chinese, we have already seen that the network of ports, pipelines, terminals, and new cities that are to connect China to Europe and Africa by 2024 (the imminent construction of which President Xi Jinping announced at Nazarbayev University in Kazakhstan in September 2013) follows the routes that came to be called, from the time of the Han and Tang dynasties, the Silk Road and which, from caravansary to oasis, from trading post to fortress, connected deepest China to Aleppo until the fifteenth century, passing through the Gobi desert, Kashmir, the peaks of the Hindu Kush, and Persia. But the new version is the Silk Road to the thousandth power, a project that, at last word, is expected to cost a trillion dollars. This constitutes a declaration of China's intent to become, by the power of trade alone, the new master of the world.

"Thucydides's trap" is much discussed in the United States these days.

Since the appearance in 2017 of Graham Allison's bestseller, *Destined for War: Can America and China Escape Thucydides's Trap*, the phrase has been taken to refer to the dangerous moment when a declining power (today the United States) realizes that a rising power (China) is catching up and soon may overtake it: this is supposed to be the moment when, like Sparta angered by the rise of Athenian imperialism, the declining power is tempted to resort to war.

I do not like the implicit messages of this theory, starting with the odd inversion of roles, where the United States plays martial Sparta and China democratic Athens.

Nor do I subscribe—because international institutions have installed some guardrails over time—to the "Ems Dispatch" aspect of Allison's argument, whereby a minor incident, such as a provocation by Japanese nationalists in the China Sea or an inopportune statement from a North Korean leader who suddenly decides to tear up the sham pact that he seemed to have reached with his American counterpart, could set the gears of armed confrontation into irreversible motion.

Moreover, I detect in the argument an unfortunate tone of defeatism. "Don't fall into the trap" is the advice being whispered into the ear of the slipping power. "Identify your vital interests; understand what your adversary really wants; and, if circumstances seem to call for it, bend."

But the most serious problem, in my view, is that, if one looks beyond the conflict with China and considers the five new kings as a bloc motivated to defy America, another trap appears. And that is the trap, not of Thucydides, but of Herodotus.

Herodotus, along with Thucydides, is the inventor of history.

He is the traveler and memoirist who, in precise and Homeric language, chronicled the war not of Hellenes against Hellenes, but of Hellenes against Medes, who would soon be known as Persians.

He is the painter of the Battles of Marathon, Salamis, and Plataea, which marked the baptism of the Greek miracle and cleared the way for the continuation of the miracle in the form of the Hellenic empires, the Roman imperium, and, gradually, by a series of moltings, the reign of the West.

But what if Herodotus's story were to have, in our own day, another ending?

What if the vanquished peoples of Salamis, Susa, and Marathon, of Granada and Lepanto, of the looting of the Summer Palace, and even of the Cold War were taking their revenge?

Saudi Arabia, as noted earlier, is supposed to be the ally of the United States; but I repeat: one must be willfully unaware to avoid seeing the troubling role that it played, according to the NGO Conflict Armament Research, in arming ISIS and helping it rise to power, as well as the exceptionally brutal murder of the journalist Jamal Khashoggi at the Saudi Arabian consulate in Istanbul in October 2018.

Iran has signed a treaty freezing its nuclear program. I am one of those who, because Iran's efforts had reached a critical threshold and the world had little choice but to bet on the virtues of compromise, were inclined to favor the accord. But a treaty is not peace. And it is not unreasonable to believe that the regime, remaining true to its nature, will continue to make the crusade against the United States and its allies a strategic priority.

With Russia, the war is a latent one, almost cold. For the moment, Russia takes care not to step outside what it considers to be its private hunting grounds in Syria and Ukraine. But the Eurasian project is there. And its goal is indeed to present an alternative to a European project deemed to be decadent and doomed. Is there an anti-Europe political party, particularly on the far right, that the Kremlin has not financed or at least supported? Has an occasion to destabilize the European Union arisen without Putin attempting to seize it, as when, during the Greek crisis of 2015, he let it be known that he was ready to print the drachmas that Prime Minister Alexis Tsipras would need were he to abandon the euro? And what can one say about the tangible military threat that Russia makes against Europe when it sends bombers into the airspace of Estonia, Latvia, Sweden, and Norway? What is one to conclude upon hearing that a nuclear submarine, on its way from Murmansk to Syria, quietly cruises through the Bay of Biscay, very close to the coast of France?

With Ankara, the war is paradoxical, because Turkey is a key link in the NATO chain. But does that not make it all the more worrisome that Erdogan should threaten to limit U.S. access to the airbase at Incirlik, as he did in May 2017 after the United States decided to step up its aid to the Kurdish resistance to Assad in Syria? What of his oft-expressed intention (most recently in November 2016, upon returning from a trip to Uzbekistan) to join the Shanghai Cooperation Organization, a forum dominated by Moscow and Beijing, unless Turkey's access to the European Union is widened? What about the lines of covered trucks delivering military equipment to ISIS, a fact duly documented by satellite photos that appeared at the time in the liberal daily *Cumhuriyet*? Or the Turkish army's outright defiance of the American army in Afrin at the end of January 2018, which resulted in the latter backing down, as it had earlier done in Kirkuk, and announcing that it would halt arms deliveries to the Kurdish rebels? Or, in Ankara that April, on the eve of yet another summit on Syria, the astonishing photo already described of Erdogan posing with Putin and Rouhani in a posture of joint defiance of the United States? What to say, even more recently, of Turkey's purchase from Russia of S-400 antimissile batteries, which are flat-out incompatible with the weapons systems of the NATO military command?

As for China, witness the steely disdain that it shows for international law; the colossal filling operations that it has carried out, since 2014, in the Paracel and Spratly islands; the creation from nothing, through massive earth-works, of new air and naval bases; the announcement on August 4, 2018, of joint military exercises in the South China Sea with ten members of the Association of South-east Asian Nations in thinly veiled opposition to the United States. These are so many signs that China is now a military power that scarcely bothers to conceal its new expansionism. And, in the face of this prospect, President Trump sounded the retreat on his first day in office by pulling the United States out of the Trans-Pacific Partnership, the multilateral free-trade agreement that had the merit, among other things, of maintaining an American presence in the region.

Things have not yet come to the point of conflict, of course.

But who can predict whether, by some trick of history, the proponents of America First might not be the unwitting and unfortunate instigators of some Marathon in reverse?

The five kings themselves do not know.

They simply see the fading away, without notice, of the colossus that had for so long held them in check.

And they believe their time has unexpectedly come.

8

Dante, Abraham, and
the War of the Five Kings

Let's be clear.

No one can begrudge a great people, proud of its great civilization and rich culture, the desire to make its voice heard beyond the borders that nature and history have drawn for it.

In principle—*in principle*—no argument can be made against a king wishing to change the order of things, to improve his position in the world, and, if he has the means, to aspire to empire.

What's more, and because it is one of the premises of this book: I have nothing against the imperial form as such—neither historically nor at present; neither in the West nor in Russia, China, Iran, or anywhere else.

Yes, there are oppressive empires.

Yes, there are murderous empires.

Yes, there have been, and remain, empires in which the colonial spirit, with its cortege of crimes, humiliations, and "administrative massacres," as Hannah Arendt put it, is almost second nature.

But non-empires, that is, states that are not empires, are by no means outdone in these matters, and we have seen at least as many misdeeds committed in the name of sovereignty as imperialism.

And, if one's criteria for political judgment are the evil that people do to other people and, as a precondition to that, the force and mastery they exert on their fellow humans, then it's worth recognizing that there is something in the nature of empire that, paradoxically, tends toward a lightening of the pressure and somewhat greater freedom.

That was Robert Musil's thesis in predicting, with Hermann Broch and other Austro-Hungarian writers in the early twentieth century, that, despite its bureaucracy, its mediocre rulers, and its reputation as "a prison of nations," the "shipwrecked" and "misunderstood" system of the Hapsburg empire would one day appear to have been "exemplary" in many ways.

It was also the view of the philosopher Alexandre Kojève, who, on the eve of the worldwide movement for the emancipation of peoples that led to the breakup of the evil colonial empires, took the risk of using the word *empire* to refer to what was, at the time, a major new political entity: the European Community, the purpose of which was to prevent the return not only of war and totalitarianism but, specifically, of colonialism.

And before all of the foregoing, it was Dante Alighieri's thesis in his mysterious *De Monarchia*, which, despite its title, was also a paean to empire.

It was the time when the Italian city-states were the theater of a pitched battle between the Ghibellines, who supported the Holy Roman Empire, and the Guelphs, who supported the papacy.

And after the Guelphs triumphed over the Ghibellines, conflict broke out between Black Guelphs (who favored maximum authority for the papacy, even in temporal matters) and White Guelphs (who sought to limit the power of the Holy See and had something akin to what we would today call a republican spirit).

Dante started out as a White Guelph.

For that he was forced by the Black Guelphs to leave his beloved Florence in 1302.

But later, in exile, he appears to have changed his mind and joined the Ghibelline camp.

Why?

The prevailing theory is that he changed sides out of bitterness, to take revenge against those who had banished him, and as the result of a switch that is certainly in the spirit of the long war between the Italian cities—which the historian Ernst Kantorowicz, in the segment of *The King's Two Bodies* that he devotes to it, describes as a primal scene that provided the model for subsequent European history.

I do not agree with this explanation.

I believe that Dante asked himself two distinct questions that elicited two types of answer that differed in substance and level.

The first related to the debate during his youth over the papal and imperial forms of authority.

And to the question of whether one or the other, the pope or the emperor, was the true heir to the virtues of the Roman emperor celebrated by Virgil and who therefore deserved the twin title of *rex* and *sacerdos*.

Dante observes the intolerable arrogance of the great aristocratic families aligned with the emperor ; he watches as Manfred, the illegitimate son of Frederick II, threatens to destroy Florence and so do away once and for all with its pretensions to self-determination; and, for that reason, for Florence's sake, he chooses the White Guelphs.

But then came the second and more important question, a question posed since the time of the Greeks: the old Aristotelian problem of determining the type of regime under which the "political animal" that is man will have the best chances for freedom.

And on this point, still for the good of Florence, the

author of the *Divine Comedy*—whom we too often forget was also a good philosopher and an assiduous reader of Saint Thomas Aquinas and Aristotle—responds as follows: in nature, the whole is ontologically superior to the part; in the other natural realm that is human social life, men will have better chances of developing their civic ethos within their village than within the family, and better within the city-state than in the village; and they raise their chances still higher when they move to the highest level and subordinate all of these affiliations to their integration within a global entity such as empire.

I am summarizing, of course. Extrapolating. And *De Monarchia* obviously does not put things in these terms. But it seems to me that this is indeed the idea.

The spirit of the isolated city-state is war (and the Italians of Dante's time were the horrified witnesses to this), since it is in the nature of a city-state to seek to impose itself on its neighbor. Compared with that, compared with the war of each against all that is the natural state of relations between free city-states, the spirit of empire offers a small chance for peace.

The experience of the city-state on its own, with a multiplicity of small, juxtaposed entities each living by its own means, also increases the probability, in proportion to the number of cities, that a tyrant would emerge from one of them. And that is what Dante himself, through his exile, discovered. The city-state, he says, is a fragmented, chaotic world, a "hall of pain," a "ship without a captain," in which the arbitrary reigns supreme. It is a system of crude, elemental power that weighs on its free citizens, stifles them, exiles them on a mere accusation, and engenders a local form of subjugation that is, of all forms, the most overpowering. Against which the spirit of empire has, at the end of the day, advantages that are not negligible even if they are unintentional.

An empire rests on a single individual, and it is easier for the human brain to accept betting on the virtue of a single person than of a multiplicity.

The master, in an empire, is generally distant and no longer possesses the means of reaching into and controlling individual lives: as a result, the absent master comes to seem like an abstraction that may even be forgotten for long spells.

Perhaps, too, as the Austro-Hungarians said much later, a political system that expands and extends people's horizons, enabling them to say they are from here but also from there, has the virtue of emancipating them even as it oppresses them. In other words, it seems as if the spirit of empire increases our chances of lowering the pressure of the whole on the parts, and fanning the little flame of civic liberty, which is what Dante cared about most. Is it mere chance (this is *De Monarchia* talking) that it was the Roman Empire, despite its infamies and corruptions, despite the brutality with which it buried the Republic, that invented the modern idea of citizenship and law? Come on, Dante concludes, addressing himself to the "Italian race," isn't it time to "let Caesar" climb back "into your saddle"? Up with empire, he insists, which, with all its faults, vices, and incontestable monstrosities, comes closest to what he called, five centuries before Kant, the "universal society of the human race."

So, Guelph and Ghibelline.

Guelph then Ghibelline, without recantation or contradiction.

And a republican theory of empire that holds beyond Florence and the Florences of the present day.

Imagine for a moment five kings with the ambition to take a step into the ranks of human universality.

Imagine the former Persia accommodating the democratic insurrections that took place in the last few days of December 2017 and early 2018; imagine if the cries of "Down with dictatorship!" and "No to corruption!" heard at the demonstrations in Mashhad, Tehran, Ahvaz, Doroud, and Tuyserkan had spread beyond the narrow circles of students and rebellious women and if they had revoked the power of the Revolutionary Guards to terrorize the world.

Imagine eternal China taking steps, even baby steps, to enter the concert of responsible nations and using the leverage it possesses to rein in North Korea or to fight, consistently and sustainably, against climate change.

Imagine Turkey changing course and, by some miracle, reconnecting with a form of Kemalism that, by some further miracle, could itself begin to come to terms with its own crimes.

If that were the case, there would be no objection to the spirit of Rumi shining beyond the borders of Iran.

If that were the case, I could find nothing to criticize in the lessons of Confucius radiating out to Rangoon, Manila, and beyond.

In other words, if the five kings were to become miraculously faithful to the noble portion of their imperial heritage, their "imperiality" would not pose a problem for me.

Nor is this hypothesis purely rhetorical.

Because I have a very clear memory, from the very beginning of the Syrian tragedy, of a "Turkish plan" that, in the context of the generalized resignation of the great powers, had the merit of at least proposing a no-fly zone, humanitarian corridors, and buffer zones, which, even if controlled by Ankara, would have permitted the victims of this awful war to have a chance of finding refuge. At the time, of course, Erdogan was already an Islamist and not nearly as "moderate" as the credulous wished to believe. But he had not yet become the butcher of Afrin. He was not yet the troll under the bridge to hell using his geographical position to blackmail the West. He had not yet taken cynicism to the point of daring to give the name "Olive Branch" to an ethnic cleansing operation. And I remember thinking, and writing, that, Erdogan or no, the "Turkish Plan" was worth supporting.

————

Let's be clearer still.

Philosophically, I have nothing against the idea of a king challenging an emperor and wishing to become an emperor himself.

I know of no argument that, in principle again, should prevent a people, whether or not they have a great civilization or an ancient culture, from defying the dominant empire.

I have too much admiration for travel and explorations, I am too fond of human diversity and its variegation, and I am too afraid of the entropy that, in the name of a simplistic version of universality, levels and standardizes singularities, not to be a little bit reassured when I see kings pushing back against uniformity.

That of course was the deep thinking of Claude Lévi-Strauss, despite the provocative opening to *Tristes Tropiques*, in which he said: "I hate travelling and explorers."

That was one of the meanings, according to the philosopher Emmanuel Levinas, of the episode of the Tower of Babel and God's anger at humanity's temptation to mount an assault on heaven, speaking with a single voice and in a common language leached of richness in the process of becoming shared.

And, above all, it is the meaning of another episode from the Bible, a very strange and mysterious episode that was one of the hidden drivers behind this book: the story of the war of four kings against five others—or, according to some commentators, of the empire against the five kings.

We are in chapter 14 of Genesis.

There are four princes named Chedorlaomer, Amraphel, Arioch, and Tidal whom the medieval commentators hold to be prefigurings of the four empires in Daniel's vision: Babel (Babylon), Media (Persia), the Greeks (whose kingdom, says Nahmanides, extended over the world after the triumph of Alexander), and Edom (that is, Rome).

Those four princes have names that are like allegories— the Maharal of Prague will call them "directions," almost "cardinal points," whereas today we would call them "paradigms." And because all four names support a single imperative of universality that must unfold in space as well as time, it is not unreasonable to consider them as one entity that may, despite their temporary fragmentation, be renamed "the empire."

Against which stand five kings, two of whom are the kings of Sodom and Gomorrah, whereas the other three (Shinab, king of Admah; Shemeber, king of Zeboiim; and Zoar, king of Bela) are complete strangers, impossible to place in the biblical chronology, and about whom the only thing we know, according to Rashi, is that their names are plays on words signifying their deep darkness. Does not Shemeber mean, as Rashi tells us, one who dons wings to fly out and fight with God?

The first bloc enters into conflict with the second.

After "fourteen years" of an "odd war" that the combatants spend observing each other, the empire attacks the five kings and defeats them on a field of battle near the Salt Sea that is "littered with tar pits."

Not content with defeating the enemy, the empire crushes the five kings and cuts their armies to ribbons, with the survivors fleeing into the mountains while their villages are pillaged.

And the kings of Sodom and Gomorrah fall into tar pits.

What do you suppose happens then?

Abraham, learning of the event, straps on his best sword, assembles 318 of his most seasoned followers, and, converted into a sort of knight of the round table, rushes to the rescue of the vanquished kings.

Abraham the patriarch, Abraham to whom God will soon say, "Fear not, I am your shield," Abraham who, at that moment, has but one real concern, which is ending up "without issue" and with "no heir to his house," makes the very surprising decision to save what is worst in humanity, its tarry dregs—beginning with Sodom.

Faced with this strange episode, the commentators have an explanation.

As luck would have it, Abraham's nephew, Lot, was in Sodom on business.

Caught up inadvertently in the battle, Lot was captured by the forces of the empire.

And, informed of this by a contingent of fugitives, perhaps by Og the giant, who earlier survived the Flood, perhaps by Michael, the angel par excellence, whose name signifies "he who is like God" and at whose wing Samael (Satan) clutches after having been ejected from heaven by the Most High, Abraham supposedly has nothing else in mind than to free his nephew.

Indeed, isn't it true that, once the nephew is freed, the gallant knight departs straightaway at the head of his band, staying only long enough to resupply for the long march home?

Doesn't he spurn the offer of a share of the spoils extended by the king of Sodom to thank him for having pulled him out of the tar pit and enabling him to counterattack?

And, once his family mission is accomplished, doesn't he abandon all of these people to their fate, insisting that for his trouble he wants "not a thread nor a boot lace"?

The explanation is tempting.

And it's easy to imagine that Abraham might have been so consumed with his progeny problem that he had no other concern than his nephew and family.

But that's not good enough.

First because Lot, nephew or not, is an unsavory character who, once saved, cannot wait to turn his back on his savior uncle and, in a thoroughly immoral gesture of ingratitude, return to Sodom, where he becomes a judge in the city of consummate evil and, as such, an agent of that evil.

But especially because Abraham, assuming he wanted to save Lot, had other ways of doing it than to side so openly with the five kings: as in a modern hostage situation, he could have negotiated with Lot's captors; he could have argued that his nephew was a collateral victim of the war; he could have paid a ransom; he was in no way obliged to start a whole new war or, once it was over, restore the five kings to their thrones.

No.

At the fringes of this biblical text lurks a much more profound, puzzling, and Talmudically paradoxical lesson.

1. In human clay the worst is mixed with the best in uncertain and unstable proportions. Of that the case of Lot is proof. For, in Lot, we have a person of quality, a descendant of Noah, of holy stock. We have a hospitable man who does all he can in Sodom to protect the angels that have taken refuge in his house and whom the Sodomites are so keen to "meet." But at the same time he is immoral enough to be there, in Sodom, oddly and culpably at ease when surprised by the empire's military operation. And also immoral enough, once freed, to, as I just said, persist in his error and, turning his back on Abraham, return and don the cloak of Sodom.

2. The law of kingdoms and empires—that is, of humanity, when from plurality it tends toward unity—is also

made in such a way that the same confusion prevails. Consider Sodom, once more. Sodom, it bears repeating, is the incarnation of evil. Sodom is that traitorous city where custom requires that an invited stranger must not leave without first being stripped of his assets. Everyone who hears or reads the Bible is intended to know that Sodom is a criminal city in which, if you get into a bed that is too big for you, you are stretched to fit the bed, and if you are too big for the bed your feet are cut off. Sodom and, by extension, the five kingdoms are trimmers of protruding heads and feet, factories for the manufacture of standardized humans, and harvesters of singularities that reset the species' counters to zero. And this is terrifying! Yet . . . What about the empire? Is the record of human life under empire really any rosier? Do we not find the same lopping and milling of singularities, the same reign of nothingness? And, when one looks closely at the three empires of which Edom is the fulfillment and, ultimately, the sole name, do they not share the feature of having worked at one time or another toward the enslavement of Israel? Babylon with its raw power, represented by its emblem, the eagle; Persia and Media, compared to a huge, insatiable bear; Greece, the panther, symbol of an audacity that went so far as to dare to negate the alliance; Rome, that beast all its own, that transcended the three others and moved them toward the will to nothingness. Really, are any of the actors less rotten than the others? And how can we avoid the con-

clusion that the empire is no better than the five kings
and also deserved a place at the bottom of the tar pits?

3. At the end of the day, what interests Abraham is neither
the empire nor the five kings as such. It is something
that lies equidistant from the two camps—that is, the
fragile, imperceptible reality of "exception." It is the
absolute exception that, in Jewish terms, can be called
radical otherness, human infiniteness, or, one day, the
coming of the Messiah. Now, the principle of messian-
ism is that it can take hold of anyone, anywhere, in any
way and lead that person to the most sublime accom-
plishments. And every commentator recognizes that
David, for example, the Messiah-king called upon to save
a human race crippled, desperate, and in darkness, is the
living proof of this principle, coming as he did from the
people of Moab, himself the issue of the incestuous
union of Lot who, after the final destruction of Sodom
and still wallowing in vice, couples with his own
daughters, who believe that the world has been destroyed
and that this is the sole means of repopulating the earth.

Translation?

While awaiting the Messiah, do not neglect any human
possibilities.

Even if you are not expecting him, close no door that
opens for humanity and the world, even if it opens in one
of the five kingdoms.

And keep in mind this secret lesson, which is also a lesson of lucidity: measured on the scale of Abraham, the good has nothing to do with these stories of empire and kings; the good, because it is an exception to history and to the standard course of things, is indifferent to the division that the empire's war against the kings of Sodom, Gomorrah, and their allies has represented since the dawn of time; and the exception that will one day arise with a force sufficient to arouse humanity, the beam of light that will split the shadows and reconcile the descendants of Noah, may very well be the pale light of Lot or of any one of the present-day Lots.

Long live the kings, the Maharal of Prague might say, after all.

Long may they live, those kings, long may they survive and even prosper, because vibrating in them, even to their very depths, is the dual potential at the center of the messianic idea, the potential for corruption or greatness, for abjection or sainthood.

And even if that were not the case, there would remain, in the rebel kings' resistance to imperial predication, in their assertion of their own predicative power, a certain something that inclines the empire toward moderation, encourages it to refine its own voice and so contribute further to the human adventure.

We can translate that another way.

There is, in the ascent to empire, a salvational note: "Pray for the peace of the empire," counsels the Chapters of the Fathers, since "if the empire did not exist" man would be even more savage and "would eat his neighbor alive." But there is, too, in empire's coruscant and metallic invincibility, in the iron corset in which Caesar confines and nearly smothers subject peoples, a pitiless ferocity: commenting on Daniel, the Maharal of Prague compared the empire to a great iron-fanged beast that roams the earth and grinds flesh.

Symmetrically, there is in the kings' resistance to imperial predication something deplorable (What a lot of wasted time and resources! So much aimlessness! Who needs these intermediate structures?) but also something precious (snippets of unique speech and voice; occurrences of high culture; fruitful turmoil and upheaval; storms not yet smothered by the empire of nothing, like the mysterious landscape of mountains and marsh behind the chilling smile of the Mona Lisa).

And it is in this sense that one may, in principle again, grant the goodwill and good faith of all those who, from Beijing to Moscow, from Tehran to Istanbul, and passing through the capitals of the Arab world to which I am bound by so many ties, claim to be approaching the realm of the universal by a different path.

So?

So, the problem is that the question today is not one of principle. The five kings are not competing to chart new paths to human universality or to reinvent human liberties outside the confines of the empire and its metropoles.

The problem is Kirkuk.

The problem is the massacre, after Kirkuk, of the Kurds in Aleppo and Afrin.

It is the plight of the Middle East's last indigenous Christians, a treasure of humanity that is now falling, like the Kurds, under Shiite "protection."

Tomorrow, God forbid, it will be my beloved Bosnia, deemed no longer "strategic" by America First, counting for nothing in the eyes of the empire of nothing, and abandoned either to the Ottomans or, via Serbia, to the new Eurasian empire of Russia.

It might be Israel, which is even more squarely in the sights of at least three of the five and could easily become, the way things are going, another "shitty little country," a troublemaker and warmonger, as a French ambassador to London was heard saying in 2001, in a European foreshadowing of Trumpian scatology.

In short, the problem is that we have five powers whose program is not to reenergize the game of civilizations but to eliminate some of civilization's most scintillating exceptions.

And, because external policy ultimately reflects internal policy, and vice versa, the types of regimes that these powers impose on their own people are no less repugnant.

Readers need not be reminded that the five are frontrunners in the repression of the freedoms of thought, assembly, and association.

They need no reminder that the House of Saud continues to be one of the worst dictatorships on the planet: no parties, no elections; apostasy punishable by a thousand lashes; a hundred opposition figures publicly beheaded each year in displays distressingly similar to the executions carried out by ISIS.

It is well known, because he brags about it, that, in reaction to the failed coup of July 2016, the neo-Sultan Erdogan tossed into prison more than 150 journalists, closed 180 press outlets, purged 150,000 civil servants, and took into custody 50,000 suspects whose sole crime was to be associated with his former ally turned mortal enemy, Fethullah Gülen—not to mention the American neo-evangelist Andrew Brunson, whom he literally took hostage.

And the same situation prevails under the dictatorships ruling Russia, China, and Iran.

This is a far cry from the benign exoticism so dear to explorers and poets.

Nothing in it remotely suggests a reinvention of the human ideal held hostage by the empire of nothing.

It has no relation to the alternative, liberating predication extolled in the West by the populists of the left.

It is just another beast that, like Edom, roams the world but is even more ferocious: a beast with five faces, each baring its iron fangs.

And in the face of that beast, in the face of these capitals of hate that disdain not only the democracies but also their own people, in the face of a terror that is sometimes latent and sometimes overt and unlimited, we must never compromise.

It so happens (the coincidence is remarkable) that the Bible contains a second story about a "war of five kings" that says essentially that.

The episode occurs in the tenth chapter of the book of Joshua.

These kings are named Hoham, Piram, Japhia, Debir, and Adonizedec; they reign, respectively, over Hebron, Jarmuth, Lachish, Eglon, and Jerusalem, which is still in the hands of the Canaanites.

Learning that the armies of Israel, led by Joshua, have taken Ai and Jericho and are on their way to Gibeon, the five kings attempt to bar the route, but Joshua attacks first, sows fear in their ranks, and, with the help of God, who casts hailstones upon them, routs the enemy.

And when, having returned to his camp at Gilgal, Joshua learns that the kings themselves have, like the kings of Sodom and Gomorrah, survived the massacre and gone into hiding (not in tar pits this time but in caves), he sends fresh troops to dislodge the kings and hang them.

It is the opposite of what happened to the five kings of Abraham.

No question this time, with Joshua, of pulling their fat from the fire.

None of the ontological leniency that, in the first war of the five kings, left open the possibility that some sparks of messianic intelligence might well be captured by the evil kingdoms.

The idolatrous passions of the Canaanite kings, their human sacrifices, the children given up to the flames of Moloch, their rains of ash and soot, all of that was too evil, the entire criminal culture presaged too terrible a catastrophe for humanity. It presented such a slippery slope (did not the Almighty find it necessary to threaten that, if the Hebrews acted like the Canaanite nations, the land would vomit them out as it had those who came before them?) that, confronted with this unique danger, a commandment came forth that is itself unique in Jewish history: break with Canaan; erase its spirit from the earth, sea, and sky; at all costs, compel mankind to leave behind the culture of Canaan.

This story is not to be followed to the letter, of course.

First because we have here precisely the type of text (in this case, a parable) that Talmudic intelligence has, since its origins, applied itself to rereading, annotating, interpreting, reinterpreting, and turning into metaphors—but absolutely never accepting at face value.

But also because of the presence, at the margin and, often, at the core of the five kingdoms, of countless men and women who—this cannot be stressed often enough— deserve our fraternal support, our friendship, and our love.

There are, in Tehran, the countless demonstrators who

have left the ranks of the murderers to engage in nonstop opposition to the ayatollahs' regime: ignoring them would make literal implementation of the text all the more fool-hardy.

There are, in Turkey, the citizens no less numerous who, at the risk of their lives, resist the authoritarian drift of the regime, such as the writer Hrant Dink, to mention only one, who was coldly assassinated in Istanbul in 2007 for having dared to suggest that recognition of the Arme-nian genocide was a question of life and death—for his own country as well as Armenia.

There are, in China, those friends of liberty and defend-ers of the Enlightenment and human rights who, even after the death in 2017 of the most famous of them, Nobel Peace Prize winner Liu Xiaobo, remain a multitude.

There are, in Moscow and Saint Petersburg, the col-leagues remaining from the time when, with André Glucksmann, we were giving birth to the New Philosophy movement: they remind me, from time to time, that, for them, the heritage of Solzhenitsyn cannot be reduced to the pathetic caricature drawn by pro-Putin "Narodniks."

And there is the memory of my last conversation with Abdelwahab Meddeb in Tangier shortly before his death. We were sitting on the terrace of an old hotel that we came to know during the period when it was frequented by American writers who were the successors of the Beat gen-eration. Meddeb had just reread the text in which Alexan-dre Kojève, many years after having solemnly endorsed

Hegel's thesis about history coming to the end of its arc, reversed himself: "No," Kojève wrote (and I paraphrase), "I was wrong; on a visit to Japan, I discovered Noh theater, the Ikebana form of flower arranging, and the tea ceremony; and I believe that there is, in these useless pursuits, these pure expenses, this snobbism, the sign of a movement of civilizations that did not stop with American utilitarianism and that would be of great benefit for America itself if she were to draw inspiration from it." We had compared those pages with Heidegger's "Dialogue on Language Between a Japanese and an Inquirer," in which the philosopher, a few years earlier, exposed his language— the language of philosophy—to the grueling test of radical otherness presented, in the East in general and Japan in particular, by the experience of the infinitesimal and the infinite, of nature and the void, of number and being. And we played at imagining what new changes might occur in thought if we brought here, to Tangier, this "clash of titans about being," if we substituted "Arab" for "Japanese," and if we contrasted the Western experience of the Enlightenment with the corresponding experiences that have shaped Arab cultures, which Meddeb devoted his life to uncovering.

If only for Meddeb's sake and for the sake of his like in China, Turkey, Russia, and Iran, we must continue to hold out our hand.

And because so many such people exist, because I have so often been able to say without the slightest exaggeration that my own freedom was at stake in Beijing, Istanbul, Moscow, Tehran, Sarajevo, Benghazi, or Aleppo, because an individual can definitely feel, contrary to the adage, as close to those far away as to those nearby, because, in other words, the idea of fraternal humanity still has meaning, I will never say that the five kingdoms are, even metaphorically, the equivalent of Canaan.

But as for the dim imbeciles who threatened Meddeb with death and who obliged him and his brothers in thought, as in Euripides's tragedy, to "worship his gods in the dark of night"; as for the cold monsters whose victory arches are built on our blind spots and renunciations; as for the leaders of those five dictatorships who aspire to outdo and crush not only the empire but also their own peoples—with them our political struggle and ideological resistance must be fierce and unrelenting. Just as Abraham's approach should be our model with respect to the five kings' oppressed people, so, with respect to the kings themselves, it is not inappropriate to remember Joshua's paradigm.

I am summarizing again.

Why is it so important to keep simultaneously in mind the two stories of warring kings, two stories that are so diametrically opposed as to constitute two different paradigms?

Because the first, Abraham's, tells us how to behave toward the healthy and holy cohort of the people of the five kingdoms. It tells us that the Arab reformers, the Russian and Chinese dissidents, the opponents of Erdogan and Rouhani are not only our brothers and sisters in humanity, but also the yeast of a West that, without them, would close itself off in Western-centrism. And it suggests that they must be given their full place at the great banquet of civilization, lest the world lose its diverse richness and eventually die.

And because the second, Joshua's, describes how to deal with the segment of the five kingdoms that trades not in life but in death. It tells us that with those who, domestically and externally, relentlessly oppose the values of democracy and law, we, too, must be unrelenting. It tells us, in other words, that with Recep Tayyip Erdogan, Vladimir Putin, Ali Khamenei, Mohammed bin Salman, and Xi Jinping, with those who support and encourage them in their designs, we can enter into all the political, economic, and trade agreements that realpolitik requires but must nevertheless remain unflaggingly aware that the war between their idea of the world and our own is merciless and uncompromising.

Abraham; Joshua. One strategy; two tactics. A single ontology; a dual policy.

9

The Brown Wave

There is one test that never lies.

In relations between powers, even hostile ones, there is an element of confrontation and an element of imitation.

There are the values of the other that the adversary rejects and those that he appropriates as if tasting early spoils.

In the war of gods and ideas to which the clashes among empires, nations, and nations aspiring to empire come down, there is a sort of enchantment that always causes the rising power to cannibalize the power then at its zenith.

Before defeating the Medes, according to Herodotus, the Persians had borrowed their taste for glory and ceremony, their model for palaces, and their theory of government.

In turn, the Macedonians vanquished the Persians only after Alexander had learned from those he wanted to defeat the elements of advanced civilization that he did not already possess—among them the art of building roads and tombs, the practice of preserving documents and observing contracts, the meaning of institutions, a plan for a common currency, the idea of shared humanity of the Asiatic and Hellenic worlds, and the art of accepting honorably the surrender of an enemy fortress.

As for Alaric, the man who sacked Rome and, in the year 410, wrote the last act of the drawn-out disaster, the striptease, the slow erosion, the sapping and withering that we call the fall of the Roman Empire, legend depicts him as a horrible barbarian who swept through the Eternal City at the head of a horde of pillagers. But modern historiography sees him as a much more complex character: intelligent; cultivated; deeply moved upon encountering the Acropolis in Athens; intensely scrupulous when, after months of negotiations with emissaries of the emperor, he entered the Via Salaria; lenient with the senators; respectful of the city's monuments—in a word, already Roman, more so than many Romans, and dreaming as much of saving the city's treasures as of pillaging them. A seventeenth-century French playwright, Georges de Scudéry, even composed a "heroic poem" presenting Alaric as a literate defender of Christianity!

In the case of the five kings, the results of the test of the mimetic hammer are devastating.

Let's widen the frame.

Let's enlarge the image—and the concept—of the empire to its Western totality, which includes Europe.

We observe the same sort of ambivalence.

The same sort of attraction, or enamored hate, mixed with the intent to overthrow.

With the important and, alas, even crucial difference that our five kings, unlike the Persians, the Macedonians, and Alaric, are less fascinated by what the envied and detested West holds that is beautiful and true than by what is least glorious and, often, most infamous about it.

AN EXAMPLE.

I am thinking of the period when a large part of the Arab world, having missed out on the Enlightenment, decided not to miss out on the anti-Enlightenment.

This is how, in the 1930s, the newly formed Muslim Brotherhood put itself forward: Nazism, said Hassan al-Banna, the group's Egyptian founder, is a global revolution that is not destined to stop at the borders of Europe; so, here, in the streets of Cairo, is another version of it! Here we are, its Arab battalion parading in Nazi uniforms and armbands!

This is the shameful story of Amin al-Husseini, the Grand Mufti of Jerusalem during World War II: thank you,

Nazi Germany, he said from the offices of the Arabische Büro in Berlin, where he spent most of the war; thank you, he repeated, between an excursion to Auschwitz and an emotional visit with the Führer, for giving Arabs the opportunity to solve the Jewish problem; thank you for "revealing the remarkable resemblances," the shared sense of "combat" and "brotherhood in arms," between "Islam and Nazism"; thank you, Adolf Hitler, "for being who you are; thank you for acting as you do."

This is how, in 1941, when Syria was eager to free itself from the French mandate and saw in the Führer a sort of savior or Mahdi in the making, the Syrian Committee to Help Iraq came together under the influence of the Ortho-dox Christian Michel Aflaq: in plain terms, this was a committee to support the anti-British, pro-Nazi govern-ment of Rashid Ali al-Gaylani in Iraq; and this is how, six years later, the Arab Baath Party (*ba'ath* meaning resurrec-tion or rebirth) emerged from the same blend of socialism and Nazism and readied itself to reign in Iraq until Sad-dam Hussein's overthrow, and, in Syria, through the Assad clan, to this day.

That part of the world, like others, had its resisters and its heroes.

Such as Mohamed Helmy, an Egyptian physician whom Yad Vashem recognized as one of the Righteous Among the Nations in 2013.

The Palestinian communist, Najati Sidqi, who fought on the Republican side in Spain from 1936 and then broke with the Communist International over its complicity with Hitler.

The many nameless Arabs who fought under the colors of Free France in Monte Cassino and elsewhere.

And Morocco's King Mohammed V, who, upon hearing from Vichy France's colonial governor that two hundred thousand yellow stars had just been delivered, responded that he would need a few dozen more for himself and his family, saying that he absolutely refused to make distinctions among his subjects and that the kingdom's Jews would henceforth fall under his personal protection.

But these were the exceptions.

The line of force, unfortunately, was as I said.

No more than elsewhere, but no less, a fascist brown pall hung in the air of that time.

Ancient history?

Not altogether ancient.

For, soon, Israel was born.

And as the struggle against Israel became the most sacred common cause of the region, machinery was set in motion that would make matters worse.

First, an argument surfaces as to why the Arab nation should pay the price for a European genocide committed by Europeans: "Why not establish the Jewish state in Bavaria?" is the thrust of the argument.

For the sake of this argument, and against all evidence, the Arab world is converted into a sort of free zone at the borders of which national socialism miraculously stopped.

Since Arab Nazism is deemed not to have existed, it does not have to be put in historical context, documented, or thought about. No work of memory, mourning, or, least of all, repentance has to be done. The result is that this part of the world, with Iraq and Syria in the lead, followed by Palestine, Saudi Arabia, and Egypt, is the only one that dispenses with the great operation of denazification that is carried out, more or less thoroughly, in Germany, in the rest of Europe, and in Japan.

As a result of which the denial, repression, and the return of the repressed take effect with the iron certainty that Freud and his successors described so well: the non-denazified Nazism, the Arab part in a Nazi revolution that one must never forget was global and thus also Arab, this intact past that is like the ruins of Pompeii (which, as Freud remarked, began to be destroyed only after they were discovered)—all of it remains hidden, whole, and very likely to be repeated.

Whence Simon Wiesenthal, Serge and Beate Klarsfeld, and others, spending their lives saying that it is here, in this part of the world more than in Latin America, that so many former Nazis are leading their second lives.

Whence Gamal Abdel Nasser who, before the war, was close to the Young Egypt Party established on the model of Hitler's Nazi Party and who, once in power, never missed the chance to recruit former SS officers and experts in political policing, prison management, and, naturally, anti-Zionist propaganda.

Whence Hamas and its charter, which, in article 32, explicitly quotes *The Protocols of the Elders of Zion*.

Whence, even before Hamas, the large number of anti-Fatah (and sometimes even Fatah) Palestinian training camps where one could find, in the 1960s and 1970s, former SS advisers such as Erich Altern, alias Ali Bella, the former regional head of Jewish affairs in Galicia; Standartenführer Gernot Baurmann, who took part in the liquidation of the Warsaw Ghetto; or Wilhelm Boerner, formerly a guard at the Mauthausen prison camp.

Whence the neo-Nazi congress in Barcelona on April 2, 1969, which included two Fatah representatives; and another in Paris on March 28, 1970, where the former SS officer Jean-Robert Debbaudt, a Belgian, placed his group "at the service of the Palestinian resistance"; and yet another in Munich on September 16, 1972, a few days after the massacre of Israeli athletes at the Olympic Games, where six hundred "delegates" applauded the Palestinians for their "achievement."

And whence today's jihadism, in which the religious dimension (the explicit and, alas, living link with Islam) must not be allowed to conceal the squarely political dimension rooted in Europe's nightmare and showing, for those who have not yet worked through it, an unsettling familiarity to national socialism.

There are two symmetrical errors to avoid with regard to Islamic radicalism and the terrorism that is its expression.

The first, of course, is to ignore what connects terrorism to Islam, to view radicalism as a product either of "poverty" or "humiliation," and to construe it as an avatar (no more monstrous than any other) of a long-suppressed desire for revolution that is supposedly being replenished within the ranks of the Caliphate: these are three faces of the lamentable "culture of excuses," which, by wrapping terrorism in a cultural context, serves to justify it.

The second is to see in it a radical otherness with no connection whatsoever to Western history and demonstrating instead a form of negativity that the tame, hygienic world in which history has supposedly ended convinced itself it had left behind while continuing to revisit it in the secrecy of dreams. (This error is the source of the most questionable fascinations, such as that betrayed by the philosopher Jean Baudrillard in a notorious article that appeared in *Le Monde* shortly after September 11, 2001, and that of people who see the jihadists as a model of vitality, energy, and courage.)

In reality, there is a connection—or rather two.

The fascination, already described, with saying all, seeing all, and showing all: it is the new law of the vaporized empire—and it finds a new application here, in the obscenity of jihadism.

And, on the European side, the insistent memory of Nazism of which jihadism is, owing to denial and the failure to mourn, the latest and most virulent expression.

———

ANOTHER EXAMPLE.

Not widely known is the extraordinary episode of the Persian Empire's name change in 1935.

Reza Shah, founder of the Pahlavi dynasty, was a friend of Germany and in time would support the Anschluss, the takeover of the Sudetenland, and the anti-British crusade.

Like the future Arab Baathists, like the Grand Mufti of Jerusalem, he believes that a new German empire is coming into being, one that will be neither holy, nor Roman, nor solely German—but Aryan.

At the same time, he knows that this Aryan myth is, in Germany, at the center of an intense intellectual agitation that is inflaming the universities, reanimating the schools of archaeology, and dividing the academies of philology and comparative linguistics.

He also knows that, in these discussions, the idea is taking hold that the "cradle" of the "Aryan" language, civilization, and race is supposed to lie somewhere between the Euphrates and the Himalayas—according to some, in the heart of present-day Persia.

And so, seeking to please the new "cousins" to whom the reigning sciences of the era are introducing him, he issues, on March 21, 1935, a royal decree that contains the extraordinary decision to rename his country: no longer shall it be referred to, in foreign capitals and international relations, as "Persia," but henceforth as "Iran"—which, in Farsi, means "land of the Aryans."

Of course, the descendants of the Achaemenids have always been known in Persian as "Iranians," that is, as "Aryans."

Of course, the word "Ariaoi" already appears, in Herodotus's *Histories*, to designate the heart of an empire stretching from the Danube to the Nile.

And Reza Shah himself, at his coronation nine years earlier, had insisted that a crier announce, in the purest Persian tradition, "At last, a man of the Aryan race has appeared to head our state!"

But you have to put yourself in the position of a diplomat posted to Tehran or heading up a major chancery and learning, on that March day in 1935, that it is now forbidden to say "Persia" and that henceforth only "Iran" will be acceptable.

You have to read the far-right French press of the time—for example, the July 6 issue of *Je Suis Partout*, which contains the enthusiastic, resounding, triumphant article by the Belgian fascist Pierre Daye titled "The Persia That Is Becoming Iran," which is devoted in large part to the name change.

And finally, you have to know that, according to the *New York Times* of June 26, 1935, in an article titled "New Names of Places: Change of Santo Domingo to Trujillo Recalls Others," this brilliant idea "was influenced by the Nazi revival of interest in the various Aryan races cradled in ancient Persia" and came "at the suggestion of the Persian Legation in Berlin." And one may well imagine that Radio Zeesen, the Farsi-language arm of Nazi radio and a propaganda machine that preached incessantly to Tehran about the alliance between the "northern Aryans" and the "nation of Zoroaster" and presented Hitler as the twelfth imam whom the Shiites have been expecting for eight centuries, missed no occasion to remind them.

That day, no one doubts that the decision, for those on both sides, is part of a major global rapprochement; that the goal is to have the greatest possible number of people chanting in unison, "Aryans everywhere, unite!"; and that this is a chance for Persians/Iranians to rise to the destiny offered to them by Hitlerism and to get on what then appears to be history's winning team.

But that's not the end of the story.

The year 1945 arrives.

The Nazis and their ideology, which were to have lasted for another thousand years, have instead been pitched into the dustbin of history.

Everyone expects the "Iranians," like so many others, to say: "OK, the game's over; Persia will always be Persia; against twenty-five hundred years of spotless splendor and glory, how much weight can one give to ten measly years during which, under the noxious influence of a handful of unworthy sons, the nation was unfortunately aligned with the black star of Europe? Let's reclaim our legacy and the good name of Persia."

Strangely, that is not said.

More to the point, that is not done.

The Allies, on entering Tehran in 1941 and forcing the shah to abdicate, tell the toppled sovereign's son and successor that the game has gone on long enough and that it is time to repeal the offensive decree. The new shah turns a deaf ear. And all the Allies get is a "neither yes nor no" that allows people to use either "Persia" or "Iran."

The new shah's prime minister, Mohammad Ali Foroughi, who is also a scholar, the author of fine commentaries on Hafez, Rumi, and Saadi and the translator of the French philosopher René Descartes into Farsi, takes the position that "with the stroke of a pen" a legendary country was turned into a more or less new country with an unknown name that people would confuse with Iraq. But no one listens to him, either. And he dies the following year, grieving what he believes to have been the suicide of a great nation.

As the issue builds in intensity and more voices around the world and in Iran declare ever more loudly that it is past time to return to the situation that prevailed before the sinister semantic coup d'état, a commission is formed in 1959 consisting of scholars, writers, spiritual leaders, constitutionalists, statesmen, and politicians. It, too, recommends closing the parenthesis and returning, once and for all, to the noble name of Persia, which in the world's mind is associated with poetry, miniatures, fine porcelain, legendary writings, and even cats and rugs—together constituting a humble and prestigious heritage from which the nation risks severing itself by choosing to present itself to the world solely as the "land of the Aryans." Power resists. Power digs in its heels. And here again the outcome is no better than an "optional" use of the two names.

And when, in 1979, the Shiite fundamentalists overthrow the regime, many Iranians still remember the mad mutilation inflicted on their country forty-four years before; there remain many who, when told that Iran must call itself Iran because that was the ancient Persian name for Persia, respond that it is as if Greece suddenly decided to demand that it be referred to as "Hellas"; Egypt, by its Arabic name of "Misr"; or China, by the Mandarin "Zhong-guo." Many of the educated people who remain in the country in 1979 object that, by this logic, one would also have to label as "Iranians" an assortment of territories that historically extended across Kurdistan, Baluchistan, Ossetia, Tajikistan, Afghanistan, Sogdiana, and more. But these are considerations that, because they can only rekindle the embers of a pre-Islamic past, are of scant interest to the ayatollahs marching into power. They, too, seem perfectly comfortable with a national name inherited from national socialism. And that is how the circle closes and how the country, even today, calls itself "the Islamic Republic of Iran."

The country's name was never denazified.

The name "land of the Aryans," with all the baggage that it carries of the power play of 1935, has wiped out the use of the name Persia.

With the result that if one believes, even a little, in the Unconscious of language and the power of names, one has to conclude that a ghost haunts Iran: that ghost is the specter of the most disastrous products of Europe's twentieth century.

This history has been recounted by others, including Ehsan Yarshater, a professor of Iranian studies at Columbia University. One can find it in Kenneth Pollack's *The Persian Puzzle: The Conflict Between Iran and America*: "There are stories told that it was the Iranian Embassy in Berlin that first suggested to Reza Shah that he change the name of the country from 'Parsa' (land of the Parsia) to 'Iran' (land of Aryans). He clearly was affected by Hitler's methods."

But I became personally acquainted with it in the course of filming my most recent documentary, *The Battle of Mosul*, when, leaving the Peshmerga to accompany a unit of Iraq's Golden Division that was staffed with Iranian instructors, I encountered—not once, not twice, but innumerable times—Shiite militiamen sporting a swastika on the back of their shirts or in tattoos, or on the windshields of their armored vehicles.

My team and I were well aware, of course, that the swastika has a history that predates the Third Reich, especially in this part of the world. But upon speaking with the militia members, all room for doubt vanished: they were, with varying degrees of clarity, also aware of its significance as a symbol of Nazism. Which leads me to wonder whether the matter of the name was really of no interest at all to the ayatollahs.

Perhaps they knew very well what they were doing in preferring, like the regime they had ousted, a name inspired by Nazis in the still-very-recent nominalist putsch of 1935 over the one bestowed by their national tradition.

And, as proof of this, I cite one last fact that was pointed out to me by Ala Hoshyar Tayyeb, one of my cameramen who, before joining the film team, was an Iranian Kurdish intellectual with a solid background in philosophy.

One day, while telling me about the Marxism-soaked adolescence he had spent in Iran before seeking refuge in Iraqi Kurdistan in 1999, he asked whether I knew which Western philosopher had the greatest influence on the early stages of the Islamic revolution.

And as I wandered into the weeds of conjecture, he interjected, "Heidegger! If you look closely, the three major ideologists of the prerevolutionary years, the three theoreticians that everyone in Iran knows counted for the most in Khomeini's circle, were Ahmad Fardid, Ali Shariati, and Jalal Al-e-Ahmad, and all three were enthralled by Heideggerian thought."

I asked him why. "Because Heidegger is the Western philosopher who is the most critical of the West. Because he is the thinker who, from the West, says that the West lost itself by getting lost in technical matters. And because he proposed the solution of breaking with liberal values. The solution did not work in Germany? OK, they said. But it might work in Tehran. Forget modernity, they insisted. Turn your back on materialism. *Dewestify*. Root yourself elsewhere. In short, reconnect with a lost origin that just happens to have the same name, since it was the supposedly common Aryan origin of Iran and Germany. That is what the major intellectuals who inspired the Islamic revolution found in Heidegger."

Once again we see, as in the case of Arab jihadism, that religious revolutions are always more political than they seem.

We should remember, in this connection, that the French scholar Henry Corbin, universally known as the great sage of the Shiite question, was also an early disciple of Heidegger who made his pilgrimage to Freiburg in 1934 and was the first to translate Heidegger into French. We should note that he traveled to Tehran eleven years later, in 1945, arriving under his double halo of historic Heideggerian and specialist in Shia Islam and meeting some of those who were beginning to organize, at the University of Tehran, seminars in "Heideggerian studies" that were the breeding ground from which the Islamic revolution would recruit not a few of its ideologues thirty years later.

There you have it.

Iran, in those years, is on the cusp of its great return to the historical scene.

Its intellectuals have at their disposition, for purposes of engaging in dialogue or of crossing swords with the West, as they choose, Diderot and his *Encyclopedia*, which devoted a large number of articles to the philosophy and mores of ancient and modern Persia; Leibniz and his curiosity; Marx and his radicality; Hegel; Foucault and his enthusiasm; Nietzsche and his Zarathustra.

Like the emancipators of Africa in the early 1960s, like some of the first Third Worlders, and like the Bangladeshi Maoist leader whom I met in January 1972 in the middle of the Ganges delta, who was still able to recite by heart, though in agony and shaking with fever, entire passages from Saint-Just's *Fragments on Republican Institutions*, they could dream, or pretend to dream, of a democratic revolution that borrowed from the best of the West.

But no.

They choose the author of *On the Way to Language*.

The one who, in 1935, a year after Henry Corbin's visit, was lauding the "internal truth" and the "greatness" of the national socialist "movement."

And there is still the same attraction, not to the luminous side of the heritage of the West but to its shameful side.

THE PUTINISTS REASON NO DIFFERENTLY. I MET ALEKSANDR Dugin, Putin's house intellectual, his Rasputin, in November 2017 at the annual conference of the Nexus Instituut in Amsterdam. Nexus is one of those think tanks (academic research, publications, symposiums) that cropped up all over Europe after the fall of the Berlin Wall and where the best of European humanism (George Steiner, Enzo Traverso, Claudio Magris, Jacqueline de Romilly, Jürgen Habermas) jostled and jousted with their opponents. Dugin looked like a fatalistic Zen priest fresh off the Kulunda Steppe. When a presenter such as myself or the American author and editor Leon Wieseltier appeared to hail from the decadent cosmopolitan world that he loathed, he would raise his eyes theatrically toward heaven and shake his head, which had the comic effect of causing his long, sparse, blond beard to wiggle. When it was his turn to speak, whether in a session or in side conversations, he would heap praise on Donald Trump, whose election was "one of the best days of his life." He let it be known that he was not uninfluential in organizing the trip to Crimea of a high-ranking "Ottoman" delegation and that this trip fell within the ambit of his grand plan for a Russo-Islamic axis passing through Turkey, Iran, and several Sunni Arab countries. But what struck me the most was this: when he tried to provide the grounds for his "sacred geography," his references were less those of the Great Russian or Slavophile tradition than those, once again, of the anti-Enlightenment strain in European thought. He would cite Johann Gottfried von Herder, the eighteenth-century German theologian and philosopher who spearheaded the

Sturm und Drang literary movement and who wrote, while traveling from Latvia back to France, about the central role of Eurasia. He would cite the German romantics who, from Jean Paul to Heinrich von Kleist, sang the praises of Russia's purity and virginity. He would cite Carl Schmitt's concept of the eternal war between the tellurocracies and the soft, liquid thalassocracies of which America was emblematic. And of course he would cite Heidegger, to whom he devoted a 2010 book titled *Martin Heidegger: Philosophy of Another Beginning*. I read the book afterward. It is hard not to hear in it a Slavic version of the "Rectorial Address" in which a Heidegger disguised as Dugin offers his services to a Führer by the name of Putin.

Nor is neo-Ottoman Turkey far from these problematics. Less "philosophy," surely. No equivalent, to my knowledge, of Aleksandr Dugin. But a hodgepodge of grand narratives, all embellishing, each in its way, the genealogy, the dynasties, and, today, the resurrection of the Ottoman Empire. There is the Mongol myth, which offers the advantage of dating national pride back to the invasion of Tamerlane's Central Asian hordes in 1402. There is the Hittite myth, which coalesced in the early twentieth century, when German archaeologists uncovered the vestiges of an ancient kingdom originating from the Danubian plains, thus establishing (supposedly) yet another Indo-European origin of the people of modern Turkey. And there is pan-Turanianism, which celebrates, in the form of ancient

Turanian warriors, the vanguard of the Ottoman armies at the time of their unvanquished splendor. The movement really took off in the 1920s and 1930s as the Turkish reply to pan-Germanism, pan-Slavism, and Iranian Aryanism. And it peaked during World War II when, with the German victory seeming a sure thing and the dismemberment of the Soviet Union seeming likely, Turks dreamed of laying claim to the Turkic-speaking Soviet republics of Central Asia. Kemalism leaned toward the Hittite scheme. Erdogan is resolutely Turanian. And, when he launches the battle of Afrin, the most seasoned observers do not fail to note, among the eight brigades mobilized for the assault the strong presence of Gray Wolves, the ultra-Turanian fighters who, in 1981, distinguished themselves by sending one of their own, Ali Agça, to try to assassinate Pope John Paul II and who since then have only grown, prospered, and merged with the most ultranationalist parties in the country. If the expression *Islamo-fascism*, which I coined a quarter century ago in *La Pureté dangereuse*, has a meaning, it is best embodied by Erdogan the Turanian.

And as for China, it has long grasped the meaning of the Marxian exhortation to change the world rather than simply interpret it. And the only philosophy that interests it is one that can be converted into technique. With the result that it has picked out from Western thought the distillation of practical philosophy that is the worldview created by GAFA. After having blocked those applications one by one, it has transformed, reinvented, and Sinified their procedures. Generalized interconnection. Massive storage of human voices and DNA. Genetic mutations under way. Artificial intelligence pushed to the limit. Development of spy software dreamed up by Americans but that no one in America had yet dared to run with. A system of social credit that obliges every citizen to have his social, familial, and even intimate activities continuously evaluated and enlists him in "elevating the honesty of the entire society." Bentham was English. But he is becoming Chinese. A new Benthamism is aborning. And its pillars are not Google but Baidu. Not Wikipedia but Hudong. Not Facebook but WeChat or Tencent QQ. Not Amazon but Alibaba. Not Instagram but applications that are infinitely more effective in terms of social control and the policing of attitudes and thoughts. I think back to the debate with Kojève initiated, four years after his death, by his friend Jacques Lacan in the preface to the Japanese edition of his *Ecrits*. On the one hand we had Kojève seeing in Japanese customs and aesthetics an Asian revival of history. On the other we had Lacan insisting that the Japanese, and by extension all Asians, "translate, translate, translate" everything that appears "readable," while inventing nothing. China changed the game. It translates, yes. But while reinventing. While metamorphosing. While producing an even more nightmarish version of Western biopolitics. And in that way, Kojève was right.

———

THIS IS ONLY A TEST.

But the results do not bode well.

One may marvel at China's civilization, as I have said.

Like other readers of André Malraux, one may well have been stirred by the adventures of Vincent Berger, father of the narrator of *The Walnut Trees of Altenburg* who, like Lawrence with Faisal or Byron with the Greeks, spends eight years serving Enver Pasha and dreaming with him of reconstituting the Turanian empire.

One may, and must, admire Persian or Arab civilization and Russia's great literature.

But one cannot deny that, in their conflictual and mimetic relations with the West, it is in each case the worst of the empire that the contemporary heirs of these civilizations are borrowing and reflecting back at us like a diabolical mirror.

Not that the West needs them to remind it of its dark side.

Hungary's demo-dictatorship is doing that very well.

As are the people of Warsaw as they rediscover the slogans of anti-Semitism and ultranationalism.

As is Austria, where a Green Party president, amid indifference from Europe and the great consciences of the country (not a peep from the Nobel Prize–winner Elfriede Jelinek), welcomes into the gilded halls of the Hofburg Palace a vice-chancellor and six ministers from far-right parties (including defense, interior, and foreign affairs). When the foreign minister, Karin Kneissl, dared to invite Vladimir Putin himself to her wedding, held on a lovely Saturday in August 2018, and when Putin led his hostess in a languorous and obscene waltz to the applause of the assembled guests and amid the flashing of cell phone cameras, a few voices were indeed raised in the Austrian press to condemn the shameful display. But so few! And how distant seemed the cries of revolt of the quarter-million protesters in the Heldenplatz with whom Jelinek, Luc Bondy, and I stood in solidarity, eighteen years earlier, when, in 2000, Jörg Haider, the founder of the Austrian Freedom Party, rose to power the first time.

And I would be the last to underestimate the fervor with which my own country seemed likely, for a moment, to yield to those evil twins, Jean-Luc Mélenchon and Marine Le Pen. The danger persists, alas. The battle rages still. Populists on both sides, even if they take great pains to put on a respectable face, lie in ambush. They are bitter, hateful, ready to pounce at the least sign of weakness, biding their time.

But they're the same thing.

We face, in the five kingdoms, a consortium of powers who draw from the same well of infamy and who cannot be bothered to put on a respectable face.

We face a de facto International—sickening, aggressive—the components of which, despite their differences, share the common trait of being attracted, as are the antiliberal forces within Europe, by the most sinister "achievements" of Western history.

These powers are at war with their own people who, when they take to dreaming of a world in which they might have the right to change their religion, or to laugh at religion altogether, or to protest being badly paid, or, for women, to live on terms of equality with men, or not to be tortured or killed, are ground in the iron jaws not of Edom but of the five. But, as they crush their own with the worst Western borrowings, they also wage total war on the other part of the West, the better part, the part that conceived the Enlightenment as well as its opposite, and which, at the very moment that fascism, totalitarianism, and colonialism were born in Europe, invented their antidotes and offered them, too, to the world.

That is another reason to oppose the five.

It is the ultimate reason for hoping, with all one's heart, that the shadow they are casting over the world may be contained.

What does it mean to be a friend of freedom today? What does it mean to remember and defend the great tradition of what used to be called antifascism? It means to invert the Abrahamic approach to the war between the empire and the five kings. It means to protect the strength that was the West against the weaker parties (weaker now, but for how long?) that are China, Iran, Russia, the neo-Ottomans, and those nostalgic for the caliphate. As in the Chapters of the Fathers, a friend of freedom must pray for the empire.

10

The Specters' Ball

Now comes the ultimate question: the ratio of forces in the field and the outcome of the battle.

I am not going to hazard a guess.

All the same, I am convinced that as aggressive as the five kings would like to appear, as abetted by the ill winds blowing across the planet, as emboldened by the faint-heartedness of their adversaries, they have major handicaps.

The first is their economic and political weakness.

Since the failed coup of July 2016, Erdogan has been a paranoid president, weakened and defensive. The Turkish economy is in crisis. Its currency is in free fall. The confidence of international investors has been lost.

Iran's mullahs can dream all they want about regional expansion. But the country's youth, the middle classes, and the population at large have been crushed by years of Western sanctions and by Trump's spurning of the nuclear agreement, which in short order will reinstate many of those sanctions. The resulting poverty has made them desperate. And they would happily trade all of Iran's adventures in Syria and Iraq for a program of anticorruption reforms.

The Saudis and Qataris are rich, but are they really ready for life after oil?

As for Russia, its industry is in ruins, its birthrate is anemic, life expectancy for men is lower than that of Iraq and Guatemala, and per capita GDP is a quarter of Denmark's and not much above Gabon's or Libya's. Not a great start for an empire.

And although China is overwhelming the rest of world with its power and hubris, some contradictory signals have recently begun to appear: a weakening yuan; slowing growth; shrinking market capitalization (nearly half of which has evaporated from its peak in June 2015); and a lagging domestic market, which has been slow to assume its role as a substitute for exports.

THEIR SECOND HANDICAP IS THAT THESE REGIMES ARE NOT well suited for the global form of influence that we are calling empire.

In antiquity, there was a long discussion about the reasons why small Greek city-states in constant struggle against one another and, a century and a half later, a young Macedonian king could have defeated the colossal Persian Empire, which had more troops, better equipment, iron discipline, and an unquenchable thirst for conquest.

The explanations were diverse.

And they diverged, if only because Sparta, Athens, Macedonia, and Corinth each had its champion whose ascent changed the story somewhat.

But, to account for the miracle, to make it comprehensible that a humble city of the Peloponnese or, in the case of Philip and Alexander, a semi-barbarous suburb of the Greek world could contain and then defeat the most powerful of empires, one word keeps surfacing: institutions.

Sometimes, as in Polybius's account of Sparta, the solidity of institutions is said to make the difference.

Sometimes, as Isocrates said of Athens in his *Panegyricus*, it is their "virtue."

Sometimes, with respect to Athens again, it is the customs and practices that they inspire that do the trick: when Xenophon presents Pericles the Younger reinventing his father's funeral oration, it is to have him tell us that the character of those who defend the laws is more important than the laws themselves.

And finally there is Aeschines, the great rival of Demosthenes, who believed that Macedonia's superiority was due entirely to the charisma, verve, and beneficence of its princes.

It is difficult to conceive, as a justification for Erdogan's hunger for power, an "Ankara Panegyric."

Hard to imagine a "Speech to Khamenei" in the mold of Isocrates's "Speech to Philip of Macedon," in which the bard of pan-Hellenism, forty years after the *Panegyricus*, extolled the probity, greatness, and moral and physical courage of the Macedonian leader as sufficient reasons for passing Athens's torch to him.

Is there a Russian Solon?

A Saudi or Qatari Lycurgus?

Conversely, can one picture a new Chinese "master of the world" having a lofty enough idea of himself and his regime to kneel at Mao's tomb—like Alexander at the tomb of Achilles in the scene described by Plutarch and painted by Hubert Robert—and whisper: "Happy art thou, Great Helmsman, to have had André Malraux and Edgar Snow to sing your praises"?

THE THIRD REASON FOR HOPE IS THAT THERE ARE FEW EXAMples in history of an eclipsed empire coming back to life.

The Persian Empire, you say? It seemed to rally against

the Arabs several centuries after it was routed by Alexander's armies. But that was the last gasp of a dying system, and the evidence is simply that two tries were needed to get the empire to give up the ghost.

The Ottoman Empire, perhaps? Erdogan likes to say that it fell sixteen times and sixteen times rose again. But those risings, like Persia's, were death throes. For three centuries, Turkey really and truly was the sick man of Europe.

The Chinese empire does seem to have endured for four thousand years. But it was a static and reticent empire, mysteriously restrained. A century before the age of exploration began in Europe, Admiral Zheng He, the grand imperial eunuch, endowed his country with the most imposing fleet in human memory but ordered the fleet to turn back when it reached the point of Mozambique, on the far coast of the Indian Ocean. And the Chinese empire was so afraid of its own desire that, after Zheng He, building a ship with more than two masts became a crime punishable by death. Was that really an empire in the same sense that China seeks to become one today?

No.

In fact, there is only one real exception.

There is but a single example of an empire that returned from limbo to put on a new face, and it did it not once but many times.

But this Phoenix of an empire, this empire repeatedly destroyed whose destruction was systematically followed by a renaissance, this empire sacked and burned before rising from its ashes, this empire whose tomb has been a cradle, whose cradle is a tomb, and whose last day, strangely, has always been the first day of a new beginning, this empire of metamorphosis that, when its head rolls, like Edom's, into the tomb of the patriarchs, perceives in the event a sign not of mourning but of work yet to be done, this empire funereal and glorious, solar and antisolar, this empire for which the good thing about death is that it is never a dissolution but always a fusion and re-formation is Edom—it is the Roman Empire whose fall Gibbon, Toynbee, Montesquieu, and others spent so much time explaining, but without ever noticing that the fall has been endless, punctuated with countless rebirths. Wouldn't it be risky to use this capacity for resurrection that is specific to the Roman and post-Roman West as the basis for a general law?

Let's consider the process of incarnation and reincarnation by which, when Rome sinks, other nations appear but then are reorganized in a new empire by Charlemagne, by the Ottonians, by the Holy Roman Empire (which persisted as a fiction into the nineteenth century), by Napoleon and his citizen empire (inventor of a civil code that was still ultra-Roman), and by the Hapsburg Empire that lends the adventure its sublime, crepuscular epilogue.

Let's pull on the golden thread spun in Virgil's Troy, which reappears in the Rome of Tacitus and Cicero; which runs through the ever-freer brushstrokes of Florence,

Rome, and Venice; which slips between the musical notes of a Germany whose sorrow, at the time, was not yet possessing a noble tongue; which shoots through the baptismal waters of French rational clarity and into the chiaroscuro of the dandy spirit of Brummell, Wilde, and Disraeli; which seems to wear thin and peter out in the joyous apocalypse of pre-1914 Vienna; but which, transplanted to the banks of New England, reawakens and reappears in the brilliance of 1945.

By that I mean the trajectory of Europe and, through Europe, of America.

I mean, for better and for worse, the terrestrial and celestial workings of that very special empire that is the empire of the West.

But that has a consequence.

The knack for metamorphosis being not a performance but the essence of this empire, its definition and its spring, there is nothing in it from which another can draw inspiration, no precept to be inferred from it, no extrapolation to be made. The exception remains an exception and can in no way be made a lesson.

FOURTH REASON.

To build an empire, it is not enough to be strong, still less to be the strongest.

Military power is worthless unless it is followed by wagons full of people capable of devising political and institutional systems for use by the conquered and the conquerors alike, as well as metaphysical and even aesthetic systems.

Augustus, Virgil tells us, was prouder of his role as patron of the arts than of his title as a judge of warring parties.

Hadrian would have exchanged all of Trajan's conquests for the pleasure of having his poetry likened to that of the now obscure Antimachus and his plans for the temple of Venus and Rome compared to the work of the illustrious Apollodorus.

Would the viziers of Bosnia-Herzegovina, heirs of Suleiman the Magnificent, have ruled so long over the citizens of Sarajevo had they not built, during the time of Ottoman splendor, caravansaries, grand mosques, the Dervish monastery in Blagaj, and the six-domed marketplace that even the Serb artillery, five centuries later, did not succeed in destroying?

And the Achaemenid rulers? Would they have deserved the title of "king of kings" if Darius had conceived the crazy idea of Persepolis solely as a temple where he and his successors would be crowned and buried, consult the oracles, celebrate the return of spring, and receive, until Alexander arrived, the leaders of defeated armies? No. In this profusion of bas-reliefs, in the Zoroastrian monuments of carved wood and caisson ceilings that struck those seeing them for the first time as an apparition, the vanquished as well as the victor felt that they were present at the unfolding of a great narrative that they had not heard before but about which they knew this: that narrative echoed the imperial deeds; it was a vivid, vibrant book of stone that told the true legend of the time while simultaneously whispering the history of humanity and of the world.

And Tamerlane? Would he have fascinated so many writers, travelers, and adventurers if they had retained of him only the images of the iron cage in which he imprisoned Bajazet or of the mounds of severed heads that he displayed in the cities he had taken? He was also the builder of Samarkand! And, in Bukhara, along the route of his conquests, there remains a Sufi monastery in memory of a devout prince who had the Koran copied in letters small enough to fit on the seal of the empire and, then again, in letters so large that a wheelbarrow was required to move the gold leaves.

And if Enver Pasha failed, it was because Turan was already no more than a bad dream and he was unable, much to the annoyance of André Malraux's Vincent Berger, to advance against Ataturk, his rival, a plan for a civilization worthy of the name.

In light of these examples, I consider the five kings of today.

I try to put myself momentarily inside their heads and the heads of their viziers.

Where is their plan for civilization?

Where in today's Iran, Turkey, China, Russia, and

Arabia are the inspiring projects? The kingly works? The great books? The twenty-first-century equivalents of the real and imaginary structures that were the glory of the ancient empires?

Where are the colonnades, the esplanades sacred and secular, the aesthetic and moral propositions, the fables capable of echoing what was said on the frescoes of Persepolis? Capable of competing with the petrified fervor of the Sassanid knights carved into the side of a mountain? With the first-century Flying Horse of Gansu trampling a swallow in full flight, the bird yielding to death as if to a caress? And where is the rival to the marvels of Attic eloquence?

Not only in the capitals of the Ummah but also in Moscow, Beijing, Ankara, and Tehran, where are the equivalents of the knowledge that led Frederick of Hohenstaufen, who wanted to wrest from the stars the secret of his destiny, to post only Arab astrologers in the eight octagonal towers of Castel del Monte, his extravagant castle in southern Italy?

A civilization, and thus an empire, exists only if it has the strength to produce poets, saints, visionaries, scholars, and characters larger than life.

The French author and editor Jean-François Revel, who was one of the few to predict the fall of the Soviet Empire, drew his certainty from the solitary fact that neither Stalin nor any of his successors could boast of having encouraged the creation of works of art, the discovery of a medicine, or the formulation of a fundamental law of physics.

Some might say the same of Western civilization, which is certainly not functioning at the level of its glorious past. Far from it.

Because history has a better imagination than people do, one cannot exclude the possibility of a Russian, Ottoman, Persian, Arab, or, especially, a Chinese renaissance.

And it is not hard to see the new China setting out to storm the world, not with its fleet (signs are that, on this point, it remains strangely faithful to the admiral Zheng He), not with its language (although the French poets Paul Claudel and Henri Michaux thought that the principle behind ideograms was close enough to modern art to be universalized), but with the inventiveness of its scientists and engineers who are beginning to rival their American counterparts in flooding the world with patents: Would not a universality based on intellectual property, technological progress, or even a quasi-monopoly on those magic materials that we call "rare earths" spell the end of traditional paradigms of power?

But for the time being, this is where we stand.

Putin, Xi Jinping, the princes of Riyadh, the theocratic ayatollahs of Qom and Shiraz, and the inept Erdogan are precisely at the point where Revel placed the Kremlin's nomenklatura in the 1980s.

One must admit that they are closer to Enver Pasha than to Suleiman or Tamerlane. And even that gives them too much credit, because Pasha was a leader motivated, in André Malraux's words, by "the call of history" and "the fanatical desire to leave a scar on the world," whereas the five kings are small-stakes players, dwarves, rulers in the mold of Augustulus.

In fact, the situation is even worse than that.

More complicated and worse: which leads me to the final reason—and, in my view, the principal one—why these five autocrats will have difficulty implementing their grandiose dreams.

I have to temper my hasty statement that they are illiterate and inept.

And, if one takes the time to listen to them, one discovers, paradoxically, a great deal of attention being paid to what they believe were the glory days of their culture.

In Iran, for example, the fundamental mistrust of the country's pre-Islamic past has not stopped battalions of scholars from being mobilized to demonstrate that the two-horned man mentioned in a certain chapter of the Koran is none other than Cyrus the Great.

In China, billions of dollars have been spent to re-create, in the middle of the Chinawood theme park, the mythic Summer Palace that was the last pride of the Han dynasty. The park already contains an ultra-detailed reproduction of the Forbidden City.

The Saudi prince who was supplanted by the current

young pretender, Mohammed bin Salman, commissioned a re-creation, in the middle of the desert, of the Alhambra Palace where Boabdil, the last Moorish king of Granada, is said to have spent his last night. That re-creation revives the original down to the last urn, brick, and crack in the walls, as do the earlier re-creations of the Prophet's quarters in Jeddah and dioramas of his battles in Medina.

In Ankara, Sultan Erdogan has built himself a colossal palace, four times larger than Versailles, where he receives dignitaries in the company of an honor guard composed of sixteen men at arms whose festooned attire of multicolored turbans, fake scimitars, and gleaming coats of mail is supposed to conjure up what the new national narrative presents as the sixteen beginnings of the Ottoman Empire.

And then there was Putin's pompous production in May 2016, following the first liberation of Palmyra, before it was retaken by the Islamic State. The organizers called it "Prayer for Palmyra, Music Restores Life to the Ancient Walls," and it featured the Saint Petersburg symphony, replicas of an ancient theater, a colonnade, the baths of Diocletian, the temples of Bel and Baalshamin, funerary towers, sound and light, ruins.

But hold on.

All of this revolves around ancient walls, ruins, theater, and reconstitution.

What these celebrations have in common is bad sets, cardboard, and lots of details that make for a truer, i.e., falser, counterfeit. Their shared feature is that they convert the times and places being celebrated into dead things drained of their substance, before which one feels nothing, none of the shimmer, none of the energy that they once radiated—things that no longer have anything to say to the people of today.

It is a frenzy of building—in a void.

Up goes a Disneyland of great temples, white palaces with a thousand rooms, sunken continents rediscovered, vast landscapes, pyramids, steles, ever-more-secret galleries, ever-more-mysterious myths—but, in contemplating all that, people must feel they are looking at a bad painting from which their faces have been purged.

And despite picturesque dervishes; despite howling Huns, Tatars, and boyars; despite Assassins and Old Men of the Mountain; despite colorful processions of priests following their new czar; despite all the Red Army choirs, Chinese ballet companies, Persian sword dancers, and neo-Ottoman Janissaries performing in the world's capitals and supposedly representing the distinctive and precious gifts the five kings can offer the world, there is in these spectacles just the right amount of overdone archaism and techno subculture to deliver kitsch—but not living memory.

Don't they have the right, you might ask, to be Persian, Chinese, Arab, Russian, or Suleiman in whatever way they want?

Yes, of course.

But to be it in these ways is to be nothing.

To reduce what you are to these collections of clichés in which, no matter how exotically you disguise yourself, the latest-generation iPhone would never be out of place, is to become a caricature or a cartoon.

To compete to be the best museum in which the only thing you still know how to do is to reproduce what you once were and once did in bigger, grander, more bombastic, and more superfluous versions, to move from object to object without ever coming across a subject, is to give in to a morbid and cannibalistic memory, funereal and self-consuming.

And this practice of planting oneself in an empty desert and reheating old words and sentiments, this clear intent to offer up to the Moloch of happy globalization the image of historic peoples who no longer have anything to show except who they are, were, and will be, this endless repetition, this continuous self-celebration, this negation of the for-itself and this desperate self-reanimation—that is not life! It has the whiff of death. It is the principle of a disorder or a cancer, in which the cells of the spirit have become mortally immortal and which, by reproducing wildly and cloning themselves, end up invading everything and giving the soul an embolism.

Granted, the empire has evaporated.

And yes, the idea of the West, having become gaunt, plain, and barren, has begun to melt in the sun like a beached jellyfish.

Or perhaps it is the other way around; maybe the West

became too big a whole, something gelatinous, flaccid, shapeless—which is another way for it to weaken, waver, and wither.

But whatever the case, the five kings have not yet taken full advantage of it.

They have not yet found the words or actions best suited to seize the opportunity that was being offered to them to fill the void.

Instead of the minds, bodies, and souls that feed true and great political adventures, they have mobilized podium dummies, wax figures, specters, abstractions, and stillborn, washed-up, faded creatures.

Zombie kingdoms.

Phantom empires.

By predication I mean a voice that strives to raise itself to the level of the universal.

By universal I mean words that can be understood not only by this or that nation, but by disparate peoples, as if they were postulates of a political rationality.

And by empire, I mean a metapolitical space open to being affected by the predication, when it arrives, of that universal.

Well, for the present, the five do not possess the ability or the will to pose the question of the universal that is required to predicate and build such an empire.

They have powers, of course.

They rule by force, as in Kurdistan, over their spheres of influence.

They are powers of earth and steel that have strewn their paths with desolation and death.

And perhaps they are and will long remain akin to the "carcasses" that Malraux said, in *The Walnut Trees of Altenburg* once again, are the only things keeping "sleepwalking people" upright amid their "ruins."

But the strength to shape human souls, a strength possessed by the ancestors whose equals they claim to be, is something they do not seem to have.

There is nothing in their defrosted immensity, nothing in their reminiscences of satraps, viziers, and ersatz czars, to suggest that they are inclined to make the grand gestures of body and soul required to take hold of the whole man, whether to subjugate or to save him.

They reign over shadow theaters.

They are thus likely to bungle their return to the historical stage.

And they seem to be drifting, temporarily perhaps, toward the tar pits from which Abraham gave them a chance to extricate themselves.

THIS IS TERRIBLE FOR THEIR PEOPLE.

Because in those realms vast numbers have thought big and dreamt even bigger.

In them are civilizations whose people felt legitimately that they had not uttered their last word and that they were about to spread their wings.

In them are living languages that have continued to resound and beat, within people and throughout their societies, like the hearts of soldiers wounded and abandoned.

And the Russian tongue of Gogol's dead souls; the Persian of Omar Khayyam and of the glorious, vanished days of the reign of Malik Shah; the Arabic of the splendid epics of the much-neglected Antar, whom Lamartine hailed as the equal of Homer and Socrates; the hymns of freedom that I heard on the battlefields of the Libyan revolution; the eloquence of the descendants of the Russians and Chinese who battled totalitarianism in Moscow and Shanghai—all that was there, all those who stirred in the night and believed the hour had come to step into the light, all has been betrayed, disavowed, done in by the five kings.

For what remains of the empire, the opposite is true— and that may be good news.

"To reign over specters is not to reign" is the dominant thought in the remnants of the empire.

These kings are merely dogs nipping at the imperial heels. They are big dogs, to be sure; in some cases, they are entire continents converted into nipping, yapping dogs. But yappers they are and noisy kinglets they remain, regurgitating old words, serving up warmed-over culture, incapable of giving it new life.

As a result, it occurs to some that Hegel might have

been right when he saw in Rome, and later in the Germanic Christian world, and later still in the nascent Napoleonic empire, the end of universal history and the last empire.

Others take to musing that the Maharal of Prague was not wrong when he saw in Edom the last word of this world.

I even encountered a neoconservative from Washington, D.C., who, as we were quarreling one day about Bush's war in Iraq, flung at me this passage from the Talmud, which occurs at the beginning of the *Avodah Zarah* treatise on idolatry: we all know, the rabbis say there, that Rome must control the world on the eve of the coming of the Messiah; but here are the nations reporting for judgment in turmoil and disorder, each displaying its particularities in chaotic and warlike diversity; here is God who, because he detests disorder, gets angry, raises a ruckus, and summons Edom, that is, Rome, to show up at the head of the line; no, no, cajoles Edom, it is I, their king, who commanded them to appear thus; I who, from the summit of my absolute sovereignty, authorized them—no, urged them—to defy me. "Live a little!" I told my subjects, the nations. "Live, shake things up, carry on as if I'm not here."

The empire, in either case, is happy.

Perhaps the empire is wrong. And perhaps its new manner of doing nothing and letting go derives from this error. But all in all its position does not seem so bad and it can go back to sleeping the sleep of victory—evaporated, vaporized, and nearly obliterated.

As for myself, my sentiments are mixed.

I am gratified, naturally, that the five bad shepherds may lose the match. I am reassured by the idea that these dashers of hopes, these sowers of death, have less chance than they think to generate a narrative capable of competing with that of the heirs of Athens, Rome, and Jerusalem. And I am convinced that a road, even a Silk Road supplemented by a belt, cannot an empire make since it lacks (fortunately) words that express the aspirations of others, a stature that invites others into a common adventure and gives it a form that all can apprehend. Their road lacks, and will always lack, the shining predication on a hill that is the prayer of empires.

But I feel too much friendship for these peoples and have put too much into the fight for their emancipation to take any satisfaction from this disaster and not to harbor, as they do, some sorrow at such a waste. There are my documentaries on the Kurdish experience and, before that, on Libya. There are the books in which I cataloged ad nauseam the stern, bare principles of democracy and human rights and, therefore, the always-open opportunity for their application in countries seemingly exotic and faraway. And there are the other books, not those that I wrote but those that have inspired me since I was twenty:

Victor Segalen's odes to the beauty of the Orient; Joseph Kessel's on the Afghan horsemen; Henri de Monfried and his Harar; Malraux on China, of course; Lawrence and the nobility of the Arab nation; Solzhenitsyn, bard of Russian greatness, whom I do not regret having called, forty years ago, the Dante of our time. That all this should end at best in still lifes and at worst in the compromise of entire peoples through dirty murders in Donbass, the pathetic rants of a carnival sultan, and a punitive raid on the Kurdish nation and its rich deposits of the salt of the earth, to that I cannot resign myself—it is just too sad.

And then there is this final and fundamental worry. The tar pits, again. When I say that the five kings have gone back to their tar pits, I am obviously thinking once more about those dark pits from the Abrahamic narrative that Rashi confirms are the counterpoint to the wells of living water dug by the Patriarchs. I am thinking of those sinkholes of pitch that, as Abraham had to know, the Egyptians used to coat their mummies—right, Mr. Erdogan? right, Mr. Putin? Haven't you, Mr. Putin, compared Lenin's remains to the relics of a saint and given yourself, via martial clichés and holy cards, the face of a mummified highlander? I am thinking, too, of the pitch-like substance that Abraham's ancestors saw used as mortar to bind the bricks holding up the hideous Tower of Babel. But I am also thinking—and, at the moment, in my reveries as a wild midrashist, this is what scares me the most—of the pitch that appears under Nietzsche's pen when, in *Thus*

Spake Zarathustra, "the animals" see Zarathustra sitting in his "pitch" and "misery." Zarathustra responds that this pitch is like all "fruits that turn ripe," which make the "blood thicker" and the "soul stiller." And I am thinking, yes, of the pitch of that dark, mummified memory, repetitive and morbid, that he calls the antiquarian memory; which, to put it mildly, prevents people from living; and which, as he was the first to have prophesized, would one day nearly kill Europe and may still do so.

For that, indeed, is what happened.

The Europeans, like the five kings, have had their battalions of historians and scholars.

They have been in the position where the sciences of the past were king, where the present crumbled under the weight of memory, and where, as in Persepolis and Ankara, everyone had more memories than if they had lived to be a thousand years old.

In other words, the historicism that peaked in the first half of the twentieth century in the form of German philology, archaeology, and philosophy was a European passion long before it settled in Turkey, Persia, or Arabia.

And we know how that worked out: the day when the "bad philologists" (Nietzsche again) began to replace the good ones, the day when the "blond beast . . . prowling round for spoil and victory" (still Nietzsche) decided to up the ante and to transpose the scholars' theories into politics, the day when the Indo-European dream whose first murmurs had inspired poets from Stefan George to Rainer

Maria Rilke began to be translated into real-world terms, the result was torchlit parades, cruel rituals, and squads sent out to manage the night and the fog.

Of course, one must not compare the incomparable.

But if real scholars were able to have that effect, if the work of someone like Georges Dumézil, the theoretician of the three "functions" (sacral, martial, economic) that he saw as common to all Indo-European peoples, could engender in readers the idea of a replacement (Aryan for Jew) that would finally free mankind of the Jewish stain, if a great archaeologist's discovery of the Altar of Pergamon and the relocation of its fragments to Berlin could, seventy years later, give Hitler the idea of reconstructing the altar in Nuremberg as a site for the celebration of black masses for races of supermen, what can we expect from the ersatz scholars who surround the five kings?

I see the specters wheeling and gliding over their heads.

I see them waiting, as specters do, for the hour when they are to assume solid form once again.

Rise and march, the kings and their wise men will say to them.

Come in from the limbo to which modernism, Occidentalism, and the love of freedom unjustly consigned you.

And, pondering that prospect, I cannot help but think of the jihadists in Mosul who, I was told, would implant themselves among the wounded and dying until they were moved into sections of the city that were believed to have been liberated. At that point, they would rise up like devils, covered with the blood of the dead, howling, and attacking the soldiers of freedom from behind. I also think of the living dead who, in ancient scenes of hell, would eagerly await new arrivals so as to pluck out their eyes, skin them, and thus renew the fraternal pact of terror. And I tell myself that even noisy little dogs, even zombies, even men unfit for empire and its predications, even those who have sunk back into their tar pits to reemerge only for brief incursions—can still do great harm and deserve to be fought with all our living strength.

Where Does the Sea Go
at Ebb Tide?

Well, that's where things stand.

On the one hand, the empire of nothing, a West that no longer knows what it is or what it wants but that, in knowing nothing, risks demoralizing those within it who still believe. This land of the setting sun that, by holding the stage and alternately preaching patience or revolt, submission or hope, the glory of the ancient world and the taste for revolution, has wound up as no more than an armless, gagged statue that seems to want to fall, slowly but inexorably, as a vulgar statue of Lenin did one winter evening or, as twilight does every evening, sighing its last light. And America, that idea qua country, the second home of every free person on the planet, a land I always saw as a good, invincible Titan—do we not have reason to fear that, in its determination to proclaim itself young, or, conversely, in its inclination to cling, like the old whore in Baudelaire's poem, to the folly, greed, and vulgarity of an alchemist named Donald, it will fall once and for all from its pedestal?

On the other hand, the five kings, pathetic yet daunting, cartoonish yet terrible, with their glorious history and the disaster they have made of it. And, in one case, China, the ineluctably ascending power that, if it fulfills everything of which it is capable, will certainly spell the end of yesterday's world.

How long have I been saying that the desert grows?

It was with those words of Nietzsche that I began *Barbarism with a Human Face* forty years ago.

But we do not always know what we are saying at the moment we say it.

Perhaps I have now reached the point in life when one begins to know.

Perhaps I have aged out of the phase where one is too busy playing his part in humanity's great orchestra to be able to actually hear the sound he is making.

Or perhaps the sound, its inflection, and the meaning that it forms have become clearer and easier to understand, because the desert has continued to grow.

In any case, now I know.

And it is a woeful spectacle.

———

So, what is to be done?

With the kingdoms of nothingness arrayed against the empire of nothing—nihilism squared, a cavalcade of kitsch—what is the right response?

First, do not give in to discouragement.

Do not fall into the trap of thinking that once one knows one can no longer act.

And do not join those around us who are saying that the game is over—their own and, by contagion, the world's.

I mentioned Spengler and his methodical "declinism."

I mentioned Hegel and his learned progressivism.

I could have mentioned Vico and his theory that history neither regresses nor progresses but turns on itself in an endless spiral.

Those are beautiful works.

They are geometric and poetic.

They demonstrate fitfully, assert constantly, speculate spectacularly, agonize over questions, respond to those questions, and conclude.

But today we know that they are wrong.

The keenest observers of history, like those who make history, know that those works are, borrowing from Rimbaud, like "absurd paintings" done by a hand "that holds the plow."

And I have read enough to know that it is possible to

construct cathedrals of thought, to write austere, granite books gleaming with intelligence and prescience, and to see all of that architecture blasted apart by a Roman horse that spooks the troops of a Macedonian general; or by the unforeseeable call of another general who, twenty centuries later, proclaims that France may have lost the battle but has not lost the war; or by another grain of sand, another pebble in history's treacherous road, another aberration brought on in the summer of 2014 by the determination of a citizen general of Kurdistan who, as the Islamic State deployed and the friends of freedom held their breath in the expectation of seeing the killers enter Erbil at any moment, decided to organize the resistance—and prevailed.

So, once again, what is to be done?

Count on the fact that books lie when they assert that history has a meaning and is moving inevitably in this or that direction, as all rivers flow to the sea.

Do not become resigned.

Believe in the power of the grain of sand, of deviation and discrepancy, of the unexpected word or deed, and of the aberrations that regularly derail the train of history.

Believe in the force of thought that never stops thwarting its own mechanical inertia: the blind Jean-Paul Sartre discovering that he had never understood all that his canonical works claimed, with such brio, to have irreversibly established; the dying Michel Foucault finding the courage to reflect finally on the courage of truth; or, what amounts to the same thing, Titian, who was never so young, who never applied his substance to the fiber of the canvas as violently, sensuously, and nakedly as in his *Flaying of Marsyas*, a picture bathed in a crepuscular light, almost nocturnal, that his old eyes strained to see.

The desert grows, and I am of little faith.

But one of the things that the past few decades have taught me is that the last word is never uttered. Never. And that a small disruption can put everything into reverse.

ONE MUST ALSO CHOOSE.

Because nothing would be worse, in concluding, than to leave the impression of equating two very different forms, nihilism and devastation.

Between the empire and the five kings there is no comparison either in essence or in scale.

Between nothing and despotism—between, on the one hand, a purposeless life under an empty, yawning heaven, and, on the other, naked violence openly perpetrated, usually in the name of a full heaven roaring in reprimand—there can be no equivalence.

And, to assert the contrary, one must have learned nothing from the tragedies of the twentieth and early twenty-first centuries.

I side with the West because there is an abyss between totalitarianism and democracy, an obvious fact of which we must never lose sight.

I side with the West because this abyss would never allow us to confuse "assassination considered as one of the fine arts" (Thomas De Quincey's formula that could apply to a state-sponsored murder carefully, systematically, and sometimes, yes, artistically planned) with "diddling considered as an exact science" (Edgar Allan Poe, a masterly parody opening with a mocking mention of Jeremy Bentham that can be read as a sinister anticipation of the swindle that is happiness in the Panopticon).

I side with the West because of the paradox that, even in the thick of the barbarous times that the human face of Europe engendered, it was also in the West, and particularly in America, where the memory of the antidote to barbarism remained most vivid; because, even when fog and night were falling, thick, rank, and unrelenting, it was in the West where the thoughts, poems, and mysteries that we could use to counterattack still shone like dew; and because, even now, as the night wind rises again over the West, with gusts sweeping away what remains of hope like stardust or the musk of lilies, it is still here, on the two continents, in America and Europe, where one finds the greatest number of resisters resolved not to let go of logic and faith but instead to inscribe thy name, O Liberty.

Bear with me one last time when I say that I have spent nearly as much time circling the globe as I have reading and writing. I have traveled to Sarajevo, Erbil, Benghazi, and the delta of the Ganges. I have revisited Harar, Aden, and the Turanian lands. And if there is one thing I have learned, it is that when death resumes its work, when people go back to killing as if they were clearing brush, when a human head, as Hegel said, has no more value than a head of cabbage, the victims turn, more so than ever, toward the West: not because it is the richest region (no longer is that true!), not because it is the strongest (the West is awfully thrifty with its strength, so afraid it is of force), but because it is the only place in the world to remember that when a single person is struck down, humanity as a whole falls.

Again: even if you are of little faith, pray for the empire.

Despite the desert, hope that, after Romulus Augustulus, Augustus may return.

One man or woman, one spark, one accident can alter the course of things: with Socrates, let us hope to hear, after the swan song and the funeral march, a cock's crow signaling the return of day.

WE MUST BE SURE, THEREFORE, NOT TO TURN THE CONFRONtation between the empire and the five kings into a war of civilizations.

Or rather, yes, but, as I have tried to say in these pages, it should be a different sort of war between civilizations understood in an altogether different sense: on the one hand, de Sade's Society of the Friends of Crime (and tyranny); on the other, the society of their subjects, their likely victims, who are our brothers and sisters in spirit and with whom we must forge links of intervention and friendship on all fronts, without regard to borders, sovereignty, and sometimes even international law.

Links against chains.

Links of solidarity versus chains of servitude.

The brotherhood of the shaken against the unholy alliance of cold-blooded monsters and frauds.

Looking back, I believe that, having posited this simple principle, having maintained against all odds that freedom has no frontier and that no form of sovereignty should stop us from coming to the rescue of imperiled people whose masters confuse the right of people to decide for themselves with the right to decide for them, is the best thing my generation did.

In those commitments there was a sense of adventure.

There was, in this patriotism of the other, a trace, a hint, of the most beautiful line in Eugène Pottier's song: "The Internationale will be the human race."

There was probably also the idea that we had at all costs to leave a Europe where Hitler had been possible and to escape from the nauseating impasse to which the history of metaphysics had brought us, even if it meant blowing it all up.

And probably, too, in the minds of some of us, there was the idea that the conflict between East and West was a fratricidal war, a war of European secession, from which one could escape only by heading south or far to the east: to Michel Leiris's phantom Africa, to Lawrence's Arabian sands, or, like the young French Maoists, to the Chinese dream that quickly became a nightmare.

And perhaps there was, at least in my case, the wish to add complexity to a world that I refused, at age twenty, to see reduced to a clash of two ideologies conceived a few city blocks apart near Hyde Park Corner by a handful of London bankers and a theorist of class struggle who turned out to have the devil by the tail.

I have no regrets about any of that.

No regrets, either, about my actions as a "committed intellectual," a role that I realize may have few claimants but that was much more appealing to me than standing around a dead tree with Vladimir and Estragon, waiting for Godot and chatting about absurdity.

And this whole history seems to me so faithful to the genius and fire of Europe that we would do very well today to reconnect with it.

Against Erdogan; for my Turkish friends.

Against Putin, Xi Jinping, Khamenei, and the Saudi kings; for and with their people, even if—especially if— they are too weak, too terrified to call upon our aid.

This morning, for example.

This Wednesday, August 15, 2018, I am going through my mail, watching the news, and reading the papers, as I still do.

Thousands of Iranian soccer fans chanting "Death to the dictator" at Tehran's Azadi stadium, an event censored by all of Iran's official media.

A collection of short stories, written by the Kurdish leader and defender of human rights Selahattin Demirtaş from the prison cell in which Erdogan has confined him for nearly two years, rockets to the top of the bestseller lists in Istanbul.

Samar Badawi, a feminist activist, has shared, since July, the fate of her brother, the blogger Raif Badawi, who has been imprisoned in Riyadh for more than six years; she managed to smuggle out a beautiful, funny letter in which she says, essentially, that gaining the "right" to obtain a driver's license means precious little if you still lack the right—without permission from your man—to work, study, or travel.

A United Nations commission of inquiry declares that it has proof that a million Uighurs, a Muslim ethnic group in Xinjiang province in the far west of China, are being held in vast, secret concentration camps and that two million others may be living in "reeducation camps."

The Ukrainian filmmaker Oleg Sentsov, who opposes Russia's annexation of Crimea and has been on a hunger strike for months, is reported to be near death.

Twenty-four hours in the life of the world—they are all there.

The opponents, victims, and future victims of the five kings.

It is with them, together, that I wish to conclude.

And it is to them all that I dedicate this book, as I write its final lines.

———

BUT I ALSO WANT TO DEDICATE IT TO THE KURDS.

The Kurds of Iraq and those of Syria.

Those whom I had to leave behind one October evening as they were going into the night and preparing for a possible return to their mountain redoubts—and those whose liquidation in Afrin I cannot put behind me.

I want to dedicate the book to Barin Kobani, the young fighter whose bright image I saw, one day, streaming in on social networks, followed immediately by another of her stripped and mutilated body surrounded by Islamist militiamen in Erdogan's pay, kicking her as the camera rolled, one posing with his boot on her bloody breast.

And I want to dedicate it to Rebin Rozhbayane, my comrade-in-arms and one of two people I consider my younger brothers from Erbil, the other being Ala Tayyeb, my cameraman, who was wounded by fire from ISIS right before my eyes. God knows I am loath to toss the word *brother* around. But no other word is as good when a man has accompanied you in an armored car, as Rebin did, through three hours of sporadic sniper fire from flaming Fazliya to Nawaran or when, with him and your friends (Gilles Hertzog and cameraman Camille Lotteau), you have spent endless hours confined in a steel shelter lost in baroque discussions of the justification for the Libyan intervention, the concept of the just war, and the ideas of Noam Chomsky. It is well-nigh impossible to avoid the thought of brotherhood upon encountering the same man, several months later, at the United Nations headquarters in New York, and hearing that he is torn between two contradictory but equally noble feelings: the shame of having been the officer who, to save the lives of his men, gave the order to fall back from Kirkuk and the honor, two days later in Altun Kupri, of having led, with great daring, the successful assault on an Abrams tank that persuaded the Iraqis to beat a retreat. And it is impossible not to think of brotherhood when, that same day in New York, at the end of another very long discussion, you feel that you may have convinced him that the honor far outweighed the shame and that he should abandon the terrible idea of reviving the practice of defeated Spartan generals, of passing judgment on himself.

Why are there Kurds rather than nothing?

How do the Kurds manage to remain Kurds when everything is pushing them to fall in behind the flags of the five kings?

That was the living enigma presented by the Jewish people for the inventors of the nation-state, particularly Hegel.

It is the mystery of exception that binds the Jewish and Kurdish people in a form of community that drives Erdogan and his ilk crazy.

And it is another of the reasons that led me to become so attached to the Kurdish cause.

I have always treasured superfluous, expendable peoples.

I have always admired solitary peoples who hold themselves at arm's length from the nations and complicate the great sorting of the human race through their unwillingness to yield and their stubborn will to endure.

For me it was first Bangladesh, half-Hindu and half-Muslim.

Then the Bosnians, European Muslims.

Later, the countless, nameless, and unburied dead of the "forgotten wars" to which I devoted an entire book.

Today, the refugees exiled from blasted lands: to them, whom we wrongly call migrants, we have a moral duty to offer shelter and assistance.

And the Kurds, all of the Kurdish peoples, who are the paradigm of the exile.

If the Messiah is indeed sitting among sick beggars at the gates of Rome, as the Prophet Elijah told Rabbi Joshua ben Levi, might he not just as well be found here among the Kurds?

If Elie Wiesel was right in suggesting that the Messiah can be recognized in the way he has, when the beggars change their bandages, of putting his own back on quickly, without taking the time to replace them all, so that he will be ready, when the call comes, to set out immediately to save his people and the world—if this image is correct, what of the perpetually gaping, bleeding wound that, as

Sirwan Barzani told me one day, was the wound of Kurd-ish destiny?

And if there is an International of law and justice, how can we not include in it, at its head, the excluded, the men and women pushed aside and forgotten? How can we fail to remember that "set aside" is one of the Hebrew expressions for holiness and that it is with these beggars for equity and law that this book had to begin and that, now, it must finish?

I am of little faith—but I believe that those maimed by the grand narratives of history, the eternal victims whose death seems to have no consequence, these magnificent and celestial cripples, count among the noble of the world.

AND WE MUST RETURN TO EUROPE.

I am well aware that this is not at all the direction of history and that the voyage from east to west, the voyage made by Troy's survivors to the shores of Italy and then by Europe's walking wounded to the western shores of the Atlantic, is supposed to be a one-way trip.

But Aeneas considered the return leg when he arrived in Crete and plague struck not only his companions but all of the surrounding fields.

He considered it again as he navigated, terrified, between Scylla and Charybdis.

And then in Sicily, at the foot of Mount Aetna and in the cave of the cyclops.

And when he was not thinking about it, the goddess was, pleading with Jupiter to let him return to Troy if he could not stay in Italy.

And didn't I just say that history has no fixed direction and that, even if it did, that direction should not be imposed on people as fate?

We face an emergency.

The desert keeps growing.

The five kings puff out their chests as the circling eagle, lazily flapping its wings, emits a shrill and intermittent cry.

And in the no-man's-land of tomorrow's world, the oppressed, the humbled, and the wretched will sail past each other like phantom ships bound in all directions.

So, once more, what is to be done?

One may hope, though without illusions, that China will send its steel junks in the wake of the fleets of the wise Zheng He, China's admiral of the western seas and leader of expeditions bound for glory and not for conquest.

One may hope—what harm can it do?—that the United States will rediscover in the wellsprings of its former predication, now almost inaudible, the strength to right itself and resume its central place in the concert of great nations.

But because two precautions are better than one and because the spring from which America will have to draw its renewal is its inner Europe, I also propose that we attempt the return voyage; that we plan an Aeneid in reverse; and that we put some life back into the exsanguinated body of Edom and Rome.

Not with the goal, of course, of creating an enormous body.

And even less a conquering monster or an additional aspirant to the universal empire.

No.

I see a political unit worthy of the name, that would have mass and power to balance the bloc of five.

I envision a level of authority that would enable it, when the Kurds of the world are being thrown to the lions, to speak with a single voice and stand up to Erdogan, Khamenei, and their Russian ally.

And my dream is to recapture the art of loving and of being seduced; the habit of the stroll and of reading in cafés; the practice, endorsed by Dante and Baudelaire, of building, repairing, and living in cities; the exhilaration of a speech (at their purest depths, the languages of Europe have never been anything other than this) that no sooner encounters the desert than it discovers the delight of filling it with song; the taste for a beautiful "now" that, when it offers itself for the taking, is an almost perfect treasure, as the grasshopper might have replied to the ant in the fable; in sum, the art and the inclination that were the voice, the flavor, and the color of Europe.

We can find that art in the trembling hand of Giacometti; in the dancing hand of Leonardo; in the pen- and plow-pushing hand of Rimbaud: in the logo-rhythmic hand of Proust, that impeded European; and in the derisive, subversive hands of Kafka, Joyce, and Fellini.

Inklings of it can be caught if one is willing to plunge into the plan put forward by Franz Werfel, during the rise of Nazism, for a European academy of scholars and poets that, on its own, would be able to forestall the worst; or into the eight centuries of tribulations, lasting to this day, of the cloak of Saint Francis of Assisi; or into any of the countless commentaries of the Talmud that search for the needle of sense in the haystack of the world.

And I have personally glimpsed that richness of spirit: in Sartre's blind eye, which twinkled with ease and irony when shaking the hand of the French president, Giscard d'Estaing; in Benny Lévy's arch look when he turned to a page in the Zohar to show me that I was not in it; on the face of Commander Massoud when, coming from prayer into a teahouse in his village in Panshir, he opened an anthology of French poetry to see if he could discern from it the future of his people—so many signs that Europe is an idea as much as a region of the world!

We need Europe as an idea.

We need Europe understood as the homeland of the idea, and thus of the universal, and thus of liberty, which the empire made possible but seems now to disdain and might, one day, prevent.

We need the sublime idea, one that is clearly a child of Europe, that we are children of the idea before we are those of a nation, a slice of nature, or a place of birth—and we would do well to set that sublime idea squarely against the toxic, suicidal, identity-based versions of the national novel festering in the five kingdoms and nearly every-where else.

Europe as a new frontier, as an inspiration for others.

New Rimbauds who, their journey complete, would head for Europe, the old continent of the future, their bags full of the misery of the Harars of the world.

Our own journey will be complete, in fact, on the day when "Grand Europeans" have managed to stand up; to hoist the sullied standard of Erasmus, Goethe, Husserl, Pericles, and Václav Havel; and to rediscover not eternity, not the dawn of summer, but the present, living, vibrant body of Europe.

Then that body, ancient and newly young, will encourage the disenchanted Europeans that we have all become to dream again.

Then, on the cutting edge of well-said, well-done, well-asked, and well-danced deeds that are another definition of Europe, will come moments of grace and affirmation that the world had all but forgotten.

And then, in the rest of the empire, Virgil's orphans will realize that they are not as alone as they feared; within the five kingdoms, a wind will rise to shake the foundations of a world whose masters had come to see themselves as the heroes of a great History set back in motion; on the rest of the planet, in the forgotten lands of the empire and of the five kingdoms, it will be said that there, at the threshold of the old continent, is a princess of the afflicted who offers not only asylum but an inner homeland for all believers in freedom and fraternity.

For those among us who are of little faith, whether sorrowfully or defiantly, Europe's self-affirmation will be an unexpected gift from heaven and from the earth.

INDEX

ABOUT THE AUTHOR

BERNARD-HENRI LÉVY is a philosopher, activist, film-maker, and author of over thirty books including *The Genius of Judaism*, *American Vertigo*, *Barbarism with a Human Face*, and *Who Killed Daniel Pearl?* His writing has appeared extensively in publications throughout Europe and the United States. His documentaries include *Peshmerga*, *The Battle of Mosul*, *The Oath of Tobruk*, and *Bosna!* Lévy is cofounder of the antiracist group SOS Racisme and has served on diplomatic missions for the French government.